P9-DHK-891

Sleepless Days

Sleepless Days

One Woman's Journey

THROUGH

Postpartum Depression

Susan Kushner Resnick

St. Martin's Press ✺ New York

This is a book of nonfiction. Some of the characters' names have been changed in an effort to protect their privacy. Other than that, every word is the truth.

SLEEPLESS DAYS: ONE WOMAN'S JOURNEY THROUGH POSTPARTUM DEPRESSION. Copyright © 2000 by Susan Kushner Resnick. All rights reserved. Printed in the United States of America. No part of this book may be used or reproduced in any manner whatsoever without written permission except in the case of brief quotations embodied in critical articles or reviews. For information, address St. Martin's Press, 175 Fifth Avenue, New York, NY 10010.

ISBN 0-312-25336-2

Design by Bryanna Millis

First Edition: February 2000

10 9 8 7 6 5 4 3 2 1

To Max, who waited for me,
To Carrie, who never let me stop being her Mama,
and
To David, who held my hand through the sleepless nights and had
faith that I would remain upright through the sleepless days

Acknowledgments

This story wouldn't have made it to the page without the motivation supplied by the Goucher College Creative Nonfiction MFA program. Special thanks go to my mentors: Lauren Slater, who ensured me from day one that there was a book here and whose brilliance helped me to crystallize what I was trying to say; Julie Checkoway, for pointing out the holes and teaching me to set the scene; and Jane Bernstein, for nudging me closer to the truth. Thanks also to Larry Bielawski for creating the Goucher program.

I will be forever indebted to Laura Yorke, my editor, for her enthusiasm in the project, her suggestions for getting to the heart of every chapter, and her talent for being a psychologist and a friend, in addition to a wordsmith. My agent, Kim Witherspoon, was enormously helpful in getting this book off the ground and making sure it stayed afloat, despite the chaos of the publishing industry. My therapist, Kate Heineman, will always have my gratitude for giving me space to cry and a symbolic shoulder to lean on while I healed.

I am also grateful to all the people from Postpartum Support International, Depression After Delivery, and the Marcé Society, who helped with research and supported my efforts to shine more light on postpartum depression.

Finally, my words wouldn't be in your hands if not for my parents. My mother, Doris, predicted when I was eight that I would be a writer and cheered me on every year after that. My father, Russ, taught me by word and example never to quit reaching. Thanks, guys—look what I did!

The only physical pain I ever knew, besides dentistry and one sore finger, was having the baby, and I would rather have had a baby every week than suffer as I suffered in my mind.

Charlotte Perkins Gilman,
author of "The Yellow Wallpaper,"
from her autobiography,
The Living of Charlotte Perkins Gilman,
written in 1926 and published in 1935

Sleepless
Days

Introduction

It's temporary. That's what I kept reading in books and hearing from my therapist. That's what the gentle women who ran support groups for new mothers and who graciously took my frantic phone calls kept telling me. It's temporary. You'll get over it. Don't worry. And by the way, you're not going crazy.

They were right, of course. The illness was temporary and I'm fine now. I didn't go crazy, but for a while I was certain that I was on my way. I went through the motions of living normally: getting dressed in the morning, chauffeuring my children around and feeding them three times a day, letting the muddy Airedale in and out whenever she barked. But inside, I wasn't right.

Like an electrical system gone haywire, with lights blinking on and off sporadically or not going on at all or shining much too brightly, nothing in my brain seemed to operate predictably. Emotions and moods, thoughts and reactions were all inappropriate and exaggerated. I cried when I should have simply frowned, trembled when I should have slumbered, and numbed up when I should have been high on love for my baby. A hundred years ago it would have been called nervous prostration or puerperal illness. In the middle of this century, a nervous breakdown. And now, the official term for that awful first year of my baby's life: postpartum depression.

Postpartum depression hit me when Max, my second child, was four months old, though it had been winding up to swing from the day he was born. It started with insomnia so bad that I'd lie awake for hours in bed between feedings, losing precious tidbits of the limited sleep allotted to all nursing mothers. Then came anxiety attacks, fear of being alone or with my kids, apathy for sweet little Max, and finally, terror that I would kill myself if I continued to lose my grip on life. There was a constant feeling of tension that no bath, no long walk, no glass of wine could cut through. I lost weight and gained mood swings. Some days I felt normal and was convinced I'd snapped out of it, but most days I felt tortured for all twenty-four hours. I would count the hours and minutes until my husband came home to take the kids from me, ending the long day of pretending to be a competent mother when I knew I was a potentially dangerous one. Then I would count the hours until I could go to bed, frantic with worry that I wouldn't be able to sleep. Finally, I would count the minutes flipping forward on my circa-1973 clock radio until daylight told me I could quit trying to force sleep.

When I was stuck in the quicksand that is postpartum depression (PPD) I didn't believe the promises I read and heard about certain recoveries. I didn't believe them because I had no proof that someone as bad off as I was had actually beaten it. I tried to uncover evidence that someone else who'd lived through similarly shaded days had survived. I embarked on this investigation with the fragments of energy I had left after taking care of two kids, two pets, and a house during the days that followed months of sleepless nights. Sleepless days, I called them, days that felt just like nights, with the same fogginess and hypersensitivity, the same sense of disorientation and loneliness one feels when gazing out the window at streetlights and moonshine in the middle of the night. I looked for survivors who could tell me how the story would end. When I finally realized that I needed professional help, I nagged my therapist to put me in touch with someone who'd reached the other side of the PPD tunnel. She never got back to me with a name, probably because most women who are through with PPD are through with it. They don't want to be reminded of their darkest days by talking to someone in the midst of it, and they don't want to waste their hard-earned mental health listening to the panic of a mentally ill stranger asking over and over again when the medicine will kick in and what does it mean that her fingers keep shaking? I couldn't find any relief in a support group because I'd succumbed to PPD at the wrong time of year. I was at my sickest in July and August of my son's first year, when the support group had recessed for the summer. By the time it started again in September, there were no veterans to learn from, only newcomers as needy or more so than I.

I looked to books for help. Someone, I thought, must have written about her experience with PPD. Somewhere between two glossy covers must be the words of assurance I craved; someone must be able to show me that she was as bound in misery as I was and still managed to untangle herself. But I couldn't find such a book, because there were none on the shelves. All the books on PPD that I found were written by "experts," social workers or psychiatrists or journalists who included all the facts on what PPD is and how it's treated, along with tips on how to cope with laundry and child care until you're better. Few, if any, had experienced PPD firsthand and if they had they didn't write in detail about their travails. Instead, the authors offered anecdotes from faceless women. *Lisa B, 34, thought she'd throw her baby out the window* or *Paula R, 27, had never experienced depression in her life.* And while these snippets of information helped me learn that many of my discomforts had allegedly happened to someone else, they weren't supportive enough. I wanted in on the whole story of a woman like me who was innocently conducting her job as a mother when she abruptly descended to hell. A real woman, with a face and a last name and a sink full of sticky cereal bowls. A woman who could give me proof—not composites and statistics—but proof that I wasn't alone and that my pain would end.

I came close to finding that proof at a big bookstore with a café in the corner and hundreds of books on motherhood and mental illness. I'd decided to buy a paperback with a baby-girl pink cover that offered a clinical overview of PPD. I clutched it between my elbow and armpit while I pushed Max in his stroller to the front of the store. I plopped the book on the counter, where it was picked up by a clerk wearing jeans and gray curls. She admired the book before bagging it.

"I wish they had something like this when I had my son," she said.

"Were you depressed after you had a baby?" I asked, shocked that someone her age had also gone through this anguish. Depression, it seems, is synonymous with pure self-absorption.

"Oh, yeah," she said, still studying the book cover. "Really bad. But they didn't have a name for it then. Nobody knew what was wrong. I just had to wait to get over it."

"But you did?"

She smiled. "It gets better," she said, her tone, her smile lines, her apparent ability to function in the world consoling me. I glanced at my son sleeping in the stroller beside me. I had loved him once, passionately, before all feeling had been snuffed out of me. Now I simply took care of him, gently but impersonally, like a salaried worker in an old-time orphanage. I wondered if I'd ever feel connected to him again.

"So, how's your relationship with your son?" I asked the woman.

"Oh, we're best friends now. He's in college. We talk all the time."

The woman in the bookstore helped me more than the

book I bought. Talking to her was the closest I came to some kind of solidarity with a fellow sufferer. I thought of her a lot over the next few months, as I got sicker and then well again. I thought of her on the phone to her boy, asking about midterm exams or when he'd be flying in for Thanksgiving. I thought of them sitting at the breakfast table together laughing over an old joke, the way close mothers and sons do. It seemed impossible during those days that I'd ever make it to where she was.

I thought I was going to die. I felt that Max, a silken parcel of smiles and coos that everyone else adored, had stolen my sanity, my strength, and every bit of joy I had expected to relish. I hated him when he smiled, *hated him,* because I couldn't seem to maneuver the same facial muscles. *How dare he be so happy,* my damaged mind thought, *when I feel so bad. How dare he mock me with his sparkle-eyed grins.* His cheeks grew plump and his fists developed enough strength to shake his Tweety Bird rattle victoriously, while I wasted away from lack of appetite and sleep.

Postpartum psychiatric illness comes in three speeds. The postpartum blues, which affects up to 80 percent of women, consists of weepiness, irritability, and moodiness. It comes on days after delivery but usually resolves itself in two or three weeks. While not pleasant to go through—I had it for about a week after my first baby—it's no more serious than a nasty spell of premenstrual syndrome. Postpartum psychosis (PPP), which, mercifully, affects only 1 in 1,000 of us, lies at the other end of the spectrum. It strikes suddenly within the first few weeks after delivery and brings with it horrifying symptoms such as delusions, hallucinations, and plans to kill oneself and the baby. Needless to say, it is extremely serious. If you're experiencing any of the symptoms of PPP, please drop this book now and get yourself to an emergency room. Nothing you're feeling is your fault. Once you get help, you and your baby will be safe and you will be well again soon.

Between the minor annoyance of the blues and the major assault of postpartum psychosis sits postpartum depression. An estimated 13 percent of all new mothers slide into this clinical depression, sometime in the year following delivery. That's more than 400,000 women a year in the United States. It can start hours after delivery or when the baby is eleven months old. It causes insomnia, mood swings, anxiety, fear of losing control, weird thoughts of hurting the baby that you never intend to carry out but that scare the hell out of you nonetheless, thoughts of suicide, and a general feeling of being overwhelmed, disconnected from everyone you love, and desperately wanting to be mothered. All those tender and nurturing feelings you expected—or felt before the depression began—are absent most of the time. You can't seem to locate your old self, though you're aware enough to know she's missing and to remember who she was.

Besides bringing on symptoms of depression, PPD can also manifest as an anxiety or obsessive-compulsive disorder. Or a combination platter of all three, as in my case. With postpartum anxiety, depression is replaced by a sense of doom. The physical symptoms of an anxiety attack—feeling as if you're about to have a heart attack or faint or suffocate—are present for most of your waking hours. Postpartum obsessive-compulsive symptoms include repetitive, disturbing thoughts that can't be reasoned away. All three versions of PPD can be treated with a combination of drugs (antidepressants, sleeping aids, and medicines to ward off anxiety) and psychotherapy.

Not everyone needs drugs to get better, but 25 percent of women will not recover without drugs, which could explain why so many women, especially of our mothers' generation, lived self-medicated on Valium and martinis. Though PPD wasn't diagnosed thirty years ago, it is often the first of many depressions a woman will suffer. A woman who has had PPD is much more likely to suffer depression again in her lifetime. The poet Anne Sexton, who spent years in and out of mental hospitals before killing herself at age forty-six, was first admitted to a mental hospital with postpartum depression. It seems probable that unresolved and undetected PPD lead to years of lingering depression and anxiety for many other women of her generation, too.

Seventy-five percent of women with PPD will get over it in a year without pharmaceutical help if they have the strength and patience to wait until their hormone levels return to normal. But as a friend of mine who suffered PPD said when she heard that statistic, "That's a pretty long fucking year to wait."

Postpartum depression isn't new and it isn't rare. When I told people I was writing this book, every female I mentioned it to had a strong reaction. My peers all knew someone who'd had the disease. "If you need to interview anyone, talk to my sister," they'd say. Or "A friend of mine had that and it was terrible watching her go through it." Women older than I tended to talk about themselves, always with nervous laughter. "Oh," giggle, giggle, "my life story!" Or "Can you still have it fifteen years later?" Snort, chuckle. I even heard horror stories of PPD and PPP. A couple who came to dinner at our house told me about the wife of a famous artist who rocked in her darkened house with her baby in her arms for days while her husband was out of the country on business. When he finally grew frantic because she wasn't answering the phone, he flew home and admitted her to a psychiatric hospital. One woman, whose children are now grown, told me her husband found her curled up in the fireplace before she was hospitalized for PPD.

Postpartum psychiatric illness has been around since Hippocrates mentioned it in 460 B.C., theorizing that it was caused by blood collecting "at the breasts of a woman" or postdelivery discharge going to the head instead of out of the body. His hypotheses reigned for about 2,000 years. In 1436, Margery Kempe, an illiterate mother of fourteen, dictated her life story. In the opening chapter of her book, she describes how she "became insane" and "despaired of my life and thought that I would not survive" after the birth of her first child. In 1838 a Frenchman named Jean Etienne Dominique Esquirol conducted the first scientific study of psychiatric illness and childbearing, proving the mental distress was indeed real. A year later, a researcher named M. J. MacCormack proposed using opium to treat what was then called puerperal mental illness. In 1847, J. MacDonald advocated the use of opium and Indian hemp instead of bleeding and restraint for postpartum patients. Finally, in 1858 Louis Victor Marcé was the first to make the connection between PPD and the reproductive organs. The illness was taken seriously and treated as well as ancient technology allowed, until 1926, when two researchers declared that mental illness after childbirth was no different from other mental illness. They also successfully wiped the word *postpartum* from the psychiatry books. The late James A. Hamilton, who started studying postpartum psychiatric illness in the early 1960s and became one of the most respected researchers in the field worldwide, called this The Great Postpartum Suppression. He lamented that the years after its occurrence were "contaminated by the needless suffering of thousands, contaminated by the blood and tears of thousands of mothers and their babies." Because of the suppression, progress in the field of PPD went the way of iceboxes and silent films until 1980. That was the year an international group of researchers formed the Marcé Society to spread and share information on the illness, and to work on preventing and treating it. Even with the renewed interest in PPD, the American Psychiatric Association didn't include the condition in its bible, the *Diagnostic and Statistical Manual of Mental Disorders,* until 1994.

It is misdiagnosed to this day. When I approached my primary care physician with an obvious set of PPD symptoms, he told me, in not so many words, that I was suffering housewife's anxiety and I needed a good vacation. He probably would have added that I needed a good bang had he not been trying so hard to appear sensitive. I started seeing a different internist after I'd recovered. When I told him that the first doctor had missed the diagnosis of PPD even though it had been all but flashing in neon from my forehead, his response was, "Glad it wasn't me. We all miss something sometime." Another time this same second doctor, a renowned internist at one of Boston's teaching hospitals, showed his obvious ignorance of PPD by suggesting that a lingering head cold, fever, and fatigue two years after my baby's birth were part of the disease. "Maybe it's that postpartum stuff," he said, when he could find no basis for my physical symptoms. "Maybe you should see a therapist."

Misdiagnosis isn't something that can be measured with precision. But a recent random survey of PPD patients by the organization Postpartum Support International found that health professionals frequently don't understand or correctly identify women's symptoms as PPD. Even so-called authorities on the health of new mothers can get it wrong. A major magazine for parents recently ran a question-and-answer column and misled its readers by discounting PPD as a cause of a particular mother's fear. In a letter allegedly from her husband, a man wrote that his wife feared daily that she would hurt their three-month-old baby and that she didn't want to be alone with him. The magazine's doctor responded that the woman probably had obsessive-compulsive disorder, which "should not be confused with postpartum depression." In truth, such obsessions and fears of hurting a baby are strong symptoms of PPD and should be treated as such.

Doctors have no excuse for misdiagnosing the symptoms of PPD as "regular" depression or signs of a personality disorder. People with all types of depression exhibit similar symptoms such as sleeplessness, anxiety, and suicidal tendencies. But the syndrome of PPD—the exact combination, timing, and course of those symptoms—is distinct.

The professionals who study PPD currently blame the illness on a combination of physiological and psychological factors. In the past, the blame has swung to one side or the other, but now,

"The definitive decision is it's (caused by) everything," says Jane Honikman, president of Postpartum Support International. Another top researcher, nurse-psychotherapist Jeanne Driscoll, sums up the indecision about the cause this way: "The state of the art is the state of confusion."

On the physiological side, hormones are suspected as the cause of PPD. After delivery of the placenta, the hormones that have built to colossal levels during pregnancy drop drastically. Hormones are thought to control neurotransmitters in the brain, which are responsible for regulating mood and keeping one balanced. Therefore, the theory goes, out-of-whack hormones can lead to mental imbalance.

But there is no firm proof that hormones are the only culprits. Other research points to psychological triggers, such as a controlling personality; a history of miscarriage, stillbirth, or abortion; a traumatic or disappointing birth experience; a death in the family; poverty and other money problems; moving to a new home; a bad marriage; or a sick or colicky baby. Some experts blame PPD on the way our culture expects mothers to pick up where they left off the minute labor started. The illness is rarely found in cultures where there is a formalized period, usually forty days, of rest and support for new mothers. Still others say a history of depression—either in the woman herself or in her family—is the biggest precursor to PPD. But why such a history tips a woman toward PPD is just as unclear. Is it encoded in the brain chemicals and hormones? Or is it passed down through abuse, neglect, or simply bad role modeling from mentally ill parents?

Driscoll and her colleague, psychiatrist Deborah Sichel, believe that PPD brings to a head a lifetime of depression. They feel that most women with postpartum psychiatric illnesses have been depressed, obsessive, or anxious before, though many don't even realize it. Once the hormonal changes of childbirth overwhelm the system, the depression erupts like water from frozen pipes.

I have no idea whether my history, my hormones, or my

stresses are to blame for my case of PPD. If given a quiz, I could check off all of the above. Though I wasn't able to admit it until I was nearly recovered, I have been mildly depressed for most of my life.

I also share with other PPD patients the common trait of depression running in the family. Both of my parents had been depressed, not to mention a grandfather and, I suspect, an aunt. The trajectory of my illness and the symptoms I experienced were pretty typical. Like many sufferers, I was a second-time mom with no history of PPD. I wasn't depressed during my pregnancy, an event that tops the list of those factors that lead to PPD, but I had experienced many of the other common triggers. I'd had two miscarriages between my two healthy pregnancies and hadn't resolved all my grief. My mother-in-law was dying of ovarian cancer, adding loads of stress to everyone in our family. I had no paid childcare or household help after Max arrived. And though my husband was tremendously supportive (studies show an unsupportive husband and bad marital relationship are common in PPD sufferers), help from my extended family was inconsistent. I was also facing a new stress: going back to work and sending Max to day care, a step I'd never taken with my first child. Any or all of these events could have made me succumb to PPD.

When I was diagnosed, I went into denial, thinking I could cure myself if I just tried harder or exercised or had a better attitude or faced my emotions or put off working or got some sleep. I was desperate to make the problem go away without resorting to drugs. Like many people, I believed antidepressants were for those too weak or lazy to solve their own problems. But the mistake I made was assuming I was in control of my brain. I thought that just because thinking and reasoning originates there I had the power to unclog the plumbing in the emotions and moods department. I was trying to fix my brain with my brain, which turns out to be as impossible as trying to fix your collapsed lung by taking a deep breath.

Finally, when some part of my brain accepted that I had neither scripted nor could erase what was happening to me, and when another part realized that my PPD was not a character flaw, but a physical illness that just happened to invade the tissue between my ears, I gave into the drugs. I started taking purple-and-peach-colored antidepressants that worked like shiny copper wiring to repair my head full of weak links. I felt sane again. I feel saner now than I ever have in my life. It was the nicest thing I've ever done for myself.

I got better, in fits and starts at first and then in a steady coast. I returned to my post as a good, loving mother. My son returned to my lap. My husband returned to work, though not without the scars of watching me deteriorate. Even as I write this, two years after my recovery, he can't hold someone else's baby. He says it reminds him too much of the months when I was sick and he was suddenly in charge of taking care of everyone by himself. My daughter, who didn't react to my depression at all until it was over, got a normal family back. And I got me back. It turns out the old cliché about that which doesn't kill you makes you stronger is true. I'm happier and more stable than I've ever been in my life. I accept now that there is no such thing as control. After a lifetime of figuratively clenching my fists in preparation for any approaching trouble, my body failed me anyway. My brain, the one organ I thought I had control of, fizzled the same way a heart or a liver can. And my recovery had nothing to do with my powers of control, either. The grace of pharmaceuticals and intelligent professionals can take credit for that. Now that I know that trouble can pop you in the jaw no matter how ready your fists are, I rarely bother clenching them at all. I'm not sure if this Zen-like worldview is the result of living through a hellish experience or of the low dose of antidepressants that continue to whitewash the angst that used to rule my life. I suspect it's a combination of the two factors and I'm actually glad I collided with both of them.

I've accepted what happened to me: I lost my mind, for a little while. Temporarily.

Postpartum depression will be temporary for you, too, or your wife or sister or daughter or best friend. You may even be able to head it off by learning from me about its triggers and treatments. But know this: you are not alone. As long as this book is in your hands, consider my arm around your shoulder. I have been where you are and you, soon, will be where I am: back in the world, in love with your baby, sane and healthy and happy. I promise. It really is temporary. I'm proof.

Chapter 1

I don't cry. So it's unusual, as I lie next to my sleeping three-year-old daughter the night before my son is born, that I taste a tear at the corner of my lip. I watch her, remembering the adventures we've shared, first child and first-time mother, the learning we've done together. We're very good at our jobs. She's avoided colic and temper tantrums. I don't yell or slap, spoil or neglect. Still, like any woman who will admit the truth, I have found motherhood frustrating and suffocating. But I have never doubted my ability to do it well. Mothering is the first thing I have ever done with such confidence, the first thing that has ever come so naturally to me.

In other areas of my life—my work as a journalist; my role as a wife, friend, daughter; even my ability to keep my house clean enough—I am insecure. I spend most of my energy doubting and scolding myself, which leaves few reserves for accomplishing much in life. I live with a constant battle waging in my head, my own civil war. One side is constantly ambushing the other for the endless failures I perceive. Later I will realize that my twenty-four-hour self-assault is a symptom of low-level depression—dysthymia, they call it—that I've suffered all my life. But there is a lot I will learn after I'm through with PPD and still more that will change about me. Even the confidence I feel about motherhood will shift. Eventually,

I will feel far more confident in most areas of my life, though far more vulnerable about my mothering skills.

But right now, hours before my son pushes through my body, I don't doubt that I will be as capable a mother of two as I have been of one. Still, I will miss this team. On dark winter afternoons, Carrie entertains herself on the carpet, building zoos with plastic jungle animals and wooden blocks, while I slouch in a chair reading the newspaper. On Sunday mornings, I draw big black circles filled with squiggly lines and she fills the spaces with color. We dig our fists into boxes of sugar-coated cereal when her father isn't around to see, and share an attraction to books that he doesn't. But tomorrow, a new player will be added to the roster. At best, he will take away the joy of our dyad. At worst, he will cause such conflict that neither of us will ever feel this content again.

I rub the back of my finger across Carrie's plump cheek and rest my chin on her hair. The tears surprise me. But there is one explanation for the magnitude of my sorrow. Sometimes, the body knows what comes next before anyone else.

The next morning, with my mother asleep on the pull-out couch and Carrie silent and peaceful in her bed, Dave and I drive through the dark to the hospital. When this pregnancy started, I disapproved of inducing labor with artificial hormones for anything but medical reasons. Those convenience births, planned to accommodate a babysitter's schedule or a husband's business trip or to reserve the most desired doctor in a large OB-GYN practice, seemed like cheating. They also clashed with my belief of birth as a natural, spiritual event. There was one way to do it, I believed, and that was to wait for God to crank open the cervix and spill out the baby. Birthdays were predestined events, not something to be altered according to the blank square in your doctor's appointment book.

I do not see it yet, but I am as rigid a woman as they come.

I am also fairly self-righteous, passing silent judgment on others and myself about personal decisions like breastfeeding and taking antidepressants. PPD will break me of this rigidity. The disease will take a brittle woman, break her, and rebuild her with flexible materials. But now I am still entrenched in my unyielding little world, where every event is viewed through a black or white lens, every person hated or beloved, every decision right or wrong.

This one is wrong, I believe, as I get ready to have my baby's birth artificially induced. But I have to get him out. I still feel guilty about it, and weak for not being able to hold out until Mother Nature pushes the start button. But I can no longer bear waiting to see if this baby will come out healthy. Before this pregnancy, I'd lost two others. They were early miscarriages—one at eight weeks and one at five—but still losses of children I had already imagined grown and happy. I mourned the first one, the one who was supposed to be born in August, with weeks of tears. The second one, who could have had the same birthday as Carrie, I didn't bother to grieve. It hurt too much to say good-bye again to a baby I'd never hold. And I didn't have any energy left for facing a loss. My mother-in-law's impending death, which hovered over us until she finally died when Max was two, sapped all my emotional reserves.

Soon after the second fetus bled out of me, an infertility specialist determined that I lacked the progesterone necessary to carry babies to term. For the first twelve weeks of Max's existence, I inserted capsules filled with progesterone into my vagina twice a day so I wouldn't lose him, too. Once the threat of miscarriage had ended, I began worrying about a recurrence of my other pregnancy complication: early labor. During Carrie's stay in the womb, I developed preterm labor—the uterus contracting before the baby is ready for birth. After holding her off for a couple of weeks with drugs and bed rest, she was born three weeks early, scrawny, but healthy. Ten weeks ago, when I first felt lower-back cramps, I was put on the medical community's version of a short leash to prevent a more severe premature birth this time. My activities were restricted to standing only long enough to make a quick dinner and driving Carrie to preschool. I was not supposed to walk if I felt any cramps, but once a week I cheated and strolled every single aisle of a small drugstore.

Despite threatening to open early, my womb stayed still, during and after the restrictions. At thirty-eight weeks, I had false labor: real contractions five minutes apart that stopped the minute I crossed the threshold of the hospital's electronic door. I walked the halls from five to eight in the morning, begging my body to start contracting again so I wouldn't have to suffer the humiliation and disappointment of going home without a baby when everyone in my family was waiting by the phone to hear news of a birth.

Through all this waiting, I obsessed over infecting my baby with Group B strep, an infection in the birth canal that is harmless to the mother, but can cause meningitis and other deadly infections to the baby during birth. Even before official labor, if the amniotic sack has ruptured, the infection can seep up to the baby. I had been diagnosed with this malady, too, when I was carrying my daughter. Once a woman is diagnosed with it, she is always considered a carrier and is at high risk during each delivery. Whenever I felt moisture on my underwear during those last weeks of Max's womb life, I imagined the sack had a slow leak, and that the infection I carry was gradually killing him.

When Dr. Laly Haines offered to put me out of my misery and induce me one week before my due date, I surrendered my self-righteous position. Haines, a bubbly woman in her early thirties who always made me feel safe with her wisdom and her knack for treating me as if I were her long-lost best friend, entered the examining room one afternoon in February holding a black leather book. She told me the next day she had free, a day convenient for her, not me. It wasn't as if I picked a day that sounded good to me. *I* wasn't tempting the fates. *She* chose my son's birthday. The sixth. Today.

. . .

We arrive at the hospital at seven, sign some papers in the admissions office, then wait on a couch in the brand-new atriumed and glass-elevatored lobby. It takes twenty minutes before anyone comes to fetch us, precious minutes, during which we have the luxury of spending time alone in this public space. Dave sticks his fingers under his glasses to rub his tired eyes and I slump down so my huge belly, covered by my faded black-plaid flannel maternity shirt, sticks up like the top of a submarine. We watch the nurses clutching car keys and the interns balancing tall coffee cups as they come on and off their shifts. These characters distract us, and inspire us to play that "who are they and what are their lives like" game. She hates all the doctors, I say about one nurse, then goes home and ties up her husband. He was a dork in high school, Dave says of a doctor, and now he drives a BMW to make up for it. There is no pain, no scribbling of contraction times, only soft laughter and impatience.

We didn't get this the last time. Labor started naturally. One minute we were watching sitcoms on a Thursday night and the next moment I was hanging from the towel rods hissing with pain. I screamed on the way to the hospital, screamed in the admitting office, screamed when I thought I would pop out a baby before Dave finished parking the car. But this time, as our daughter awaits a sibling at home and our son lives his last moments of fish life inside my uterine aquarium, we are civilized, controlled.

We are, after all, veterans. We believe we know what's ahead of us and are sure we can handle it. Dave expects it to be as easy as I do.

"It'll be like the three of us plus a baby," he says. "Nothing different."

Finally, a nurse approaches. She asks if she can take me to the room first, then retrieve Dave. I don't like this separation, but I follow her into a gently lit hospital room with a clear plastic infant crib in one corner and a rocking chair in the other. She sits down on the single bed in the middle of the room and pats the space beside her white polyester thigh, inviting me to join her. I obey, wondering what this intimate positioning has to do with my appointment to have a baby. I want to get down to business: strip, tie on a gown, give blood samples, take laboratory-manufactured hormones, and shove out a son. I don't want to chat, which she seems to sense.

"We ask everyone to do this," she explains. "It'll just take a second."

She asks about my due date and my pregnancy history, facts she could easily glean from the file she's holding, then gets down to the real reason for the solo trip: "Do you ever feel afraid in your relationship that your husband will hurt you?"

"No," I answer, the real part of me shocked that she would think such a thing about my tender husband, the social activist in me glad that the hospital has set up this system to protect women who could answer the question affirmatively. They worry that the mother will leave with a baby and put both of them in danger, as if that is the only danger the pair could encounter. If the nurse had asked the opposite question, "Are you confident in your relationship that your husband will save you?" I would have said yes. I would have been right.

She brightens up, now that the uncomfortable question has been answered comfortably, and hands me a cotton frock.

"I'll go get your husband," she says. "And your labor and delivery nurse will be Barb today."

"It's not you?" I ask. I've been worried about what my nurse, the one professional who will spend most of the labor with me, will be like. It's been said that a good or bad nurse can make or break the birthing experience. This one seems kind. I'd like to keep her.

"No, I just do check-in," she says with a smile. "You can change in the bathroom."

Barb, who tells us that she is divorced and about to go on vacation to Florida, is as cold and bitter as the weather she's escaping. She is tall and thin, with bottle blond hair that is blunted at her cheekbones. Because I am being induced and because I will need antibiotics during labor to fight the strep B, she prepares an IV line for my hand. "I've never had one before," I tell her, "I'm nervous." She jams the needle and plastic tube into my skin without looking at me. After the fluids have started flowing and I am strapped to a fetal monitor, Dr. Haines comes in to break my water. She prods the sack with a white plastic stick that looks like a knitting needle, pushing and twisting at the tough membrane until finally I feel hot liquid gush over my thighs and rear. Like someone with bladder control problems, I don't feel it coming out or have the ability to stop it. It seems endless. It keeps coming and coming and I panic, realizing I have no say over what my body is doing.

Contractions, sharp and sudden, begin soon after Barb and the doctor leave. Barb stands at the nurse's station, talking, while I scream into a pillow and beg for painkillers.

"It's too soon," she says, annoyed, as she looks at the strip of paper regurgitated from the fetal monitor that indicates the closeness of contractions. "You have to wait longer."

When she leaves, I ask Dave if he can convince her to get Dr. Haines. My husband is a short, trim man with a self-described face of a rabbi. He has salt-and-pepper hair that gets saltier by the month and sea blue eyes that hide behind strong glasses. He is the type of person that everyone loves. His manner—sweet, genuine, funny, and devoid of bitterness—draws people to him. I don't think he has ever had or will ever have any enemies. I joke that he is a new soul, free of the baggage from a previous life that causes shadows and dark crevices in most of us. He is as strong, confident, and cool as I am flailing and emotional, which is probably why we get along so well. It also helps tremendously that he brings me water from downstairs in the middle of the night when I'm thirsty and listens to me worry whenever I ask for his ear, all without ever stepping on my independence. Sure, he has some flaws, such as not being honest about his anger, extreme sloppiness, and possibly being the slowest man on earth when it comes to getting dressed or preparing a meal. But for the most part, he's golden. It's this personality that makes it so easy for him to talk the steely nurse into getting my doctor without offending her.

Dr. Haines sticks a gloved finger inside me and orders Barb to shoot a syringe full of the narcotic Nubian into my IV line. I'm getting close.

I start to feel woozy and heavy and weak and before long I see everything twice. Double vision nauseates me, so I close my eyes, hold Dave's hand, and ask him to tell me when he sees a contraction starting on the monitor.

"Here comes one," he says, over and over, in a voice both excited and soothing.

"Oh, yeah," I slur. "It hurts. It hurts. Okay it's better now."

I don't scream anymore, because I can't feel the pain directly now. The contractions feel the same, but my brain doesn't register it as pain, or signal anything that reacts to pain to jump into action. The Nubian is like a cotton ball jammed into an eardrum: sounds come through, but not strong enough to elicit a response.

The drug lasts about ninety minutes. As it wears off, and the pain and my mind become clearer, Dr. Haines measures my stretched cervix and victoriously announces that it's time to push. Barb and Dave each grab one of my thighs and pull them toward my head so I am spread as wide as possible. Dr. Haines stands in front of my vagina as if she's about to conduct an orchestra and orders me to push. Suddenly that forgetfulness that Mother Nature created in mothers to further the species melts away. I remember everything about Carrie's birth, particularly the sensation of being turned inside out like a freshly washed sock while pushing her out of my body without the crutch of drugs. I realize I can't possibly go through that again. *How can I get out of here?* I think, trying to come up with a plan. *How can I slip out so these three don't notice?*

They keep bossing me around, as impatient and unsympathetic as basketball coaches, so I obey. I push and push, pretending I'm trying as hard as I can, until out slides a little poop. I am so embarrassed that I shout, "Did I just take a shit?," and someone tells me yes, not to worry about it. Then I push with more spirit until I feel something tear. Not in the spot I'd expected, between my vagina and anus, but in the front of my body, near my urethra. I feel as if I am splitting, that something inside is tearing and that when the baby's head comes out, it will keep tearing right up the front of me, like a zipper.

Finally, the baby arrives, leaving only small, predictable sections of my bottom tattered. He is blue and motionless with part of the amniotic sack wrapped over him. Dave says he looks like a space creature. He is terrified because he thinks the baby is dead, though he doesn't tell me this until months later. It is the Resnick trademark to spare loved ones any ugliness. All of Dave's family members protect one another from the truth. I once called it lying, but now I see it as a form of love.

They take Max to an isolette and rough him up a little to get him to breathe, put drops in his eyes, then bring him back to me. There is no magic moment of bonding. Dave cries and Dr. Haines praises me for getting it over with so quickly, but all I can think is that I have go to the bathroom. There are photos of me holding Max and talking on the phone and smiling, but I don't remember making those calls or smiling those smiles.

It is said that a traumatic or dissatisfying birth experience is one of the factors that can lead to postpartum depression. I gave birth to Carrie with the assistance of a nurse-midwife, a hot shower to tame the pain, and a nearly dark hospital room in which to greet my new child. After the pain and fear subsided, I felt I had accomplished something courageous and breathtaking. Max's high-tech birth was defined by bright lights, IV tubes, straps that tethered me to the fetal monitor next to the bed, stupefying medication, and a heartless nurse. After he arrived, I felt as if I'd been through a harsh medical procedure. Had I experienced another noninduced, low-tech delivery, I wonder, would I have avoided PPD?

A few minutes after birthing Max, we load my overnight bag, coat, pocketbook, and me into a wheelchair. Max, wrapped in a stripped flannel blanket and wearing a matching striped cap, lies in my arms. I still feel woozy and unstable from the drugs, as if I am about to collapse. I worry that I'll let him roll off my lap onto the hallway or down the elevator shaft as we ride to another floor and our permanent room.

After a nurse bathes and diapers Max, and changes the pad and ice pack between my legs, Dave goes home to get Carrie. When he brings her back, there are presents to open. After peering quickly at the being who will later become her beloved playmate, she tears through the wrapping paper. My tiny girl suddenly looks huge to me. She wears a T-shirt that declares *I'm the Big Sister* over her pink turtleneck. Even her new Richard Scarry figurines seem so-phisticated compared to the stuffed gray horse she gives to Max.

After some playing on the bed and reminding her father that she was promised ice cream when the baby was born, they leave. My first obsession starts. Though we knew we would name our son Max as soon as we learned his sex (Dave had made me promise to name our first boy after his grandfather the Russian fruit peddler during our second date, and had held me to it), it is up to me to pick a middle name. I know I want something that starts with J. From a long list, Justin, Jacob, Julian, and James have made the final cut. I love them all, but each has a drawback. Though four of his great-great-grandfathers were named Jacob, I find it too eth-nic and predictable, especially next to Max. Dave hates the name Justin. Julian is the middle name of another boy named Max in our small town and James is one syllable too short. The birth certificate office needs the name before I leave the hospital in two days, so I spend every moment I am alone over the next few days obsessing about the decision. Order always gives me a sense of control when

I am insecure or anxious, so for my entire hospitalization, I keep straightening my room, then returning to the list of names and trying each one out in my head. I throw out wrappers from pain pills and stool softeners, toss soiled newborn T-shirts in the hamper, change the pad on the diapering cart, push the flowers my mother sent to the center of the window sill, place my slippers next to the bed, climb under the sheets and recite: Max James, Max Justin, Max Julian, Max Jacob over and over until somebody calls or visits. It is so important and final, so crucial that the name be perfect. But I can't rest on one combination. I've often had trouble making important decisions, and I've been pondering this middle name question for months, but it's never possessed me like this. My mind runs in circles, day and night, until the birth certificate lady calls and in a panic I choose the safest middle name, Jacob.

Obsessing isn't the only postpartum symptom that's unique to this birth. After Carrie's arrival, there was celebration, visitors, a bouquet of pink balloons tied to a chair in the hospital room. This time there is on-and-off weeping. I blame it on the loneliness. Since Dave has to spend time at home with Carrie, and she's bored after a few minutes in the hospital, he only visits for a couple of hours each day. Except for mandatory blood pressure checks twice a shift, the nurses neglect me because I'm a second-timer. My best friend, Kelly, can't visit me because there's a big snowstorm predicted and her babysitter cancels. Dave tells me the storm will be so bad that he doesn't even know if he'll be able to pick us up after we're to be discharged.

Late in the afternoon, one day after Max's birth, I wander the circular hallway of the ward, looking for someone to talk to. We aren't allowed to carry our babies in the hallway, so I push him in his Plexiglas rolling crib. I peek into rooms filled with happy relatives and pass couples walking their babies together, the father with one arm around the mother and the other pushing the crib. No one seems to see us, though there are tears in my eyes and, I imagine, a beseeching look on my face. I walk to the dead end of a hallway, stand by a window, and watch the snow whip past me. It blows the coat off the back of a lone pedestrian down on the street, and covers the roads so thoroughly that curbs and fire hydrants can't be distinguished. I look at Max, who is sleeping, and I try to feel how special this should be, just me and my new, new baby against the world. But instead I feel homesick and more alone than I have in years.

As a little girl, I was always lonely. In second grade I wrote and illustrated my first book. The stick-figure girl on the cover was frowning. Inside, I told the story of a girl who is rejected by her entire family. Everyone is too busy to play with her until her father comes home and takes her to the park on his shoulders. My teacher entered the book in a contest, but it didn't win. When I was thirteen I started collecting poems that other girls published in *Teen* magazine. I pasted them into a book I made out of loose-leaf notebook paper and kitchen string. On one page I pasted a poem I'd written myself, in blue magic marker.

"I dream, and make all bad things good again. But when I come back to reality, nothing has changed. Except after I dream, I have more hope and courage to really make the bad things good again."

My parents sent me to therapists when they couldn't deal with my inexplicable sadness. It felt like punishment, as if they were saying, *We couldn't fix you and you couldn't fix you, so now you must be fixed by a stranger.* I did not think I was a normal kid. I was scared of everything. I always had stomachaches. No one I knew went to therapy. No one I knew appeared to be as sad as I was. Then the therapy would make me feel better, which meant I needed it, which made me feel weirder than ever.

A few relationships were able to take away the loneliness temporarily. I dated another depressive for many years. He, like I, didn't know he was depressed. He had never been diagnosed either, despite so many obvious symptoms that I catalog when I face my own depression. Our relationship was stormy, filled with tears and fights, neediness and fury. I felt less odd with this man because he was so much like me. But we were two negatives and we dragged each other down until I left him.

I finally shed loneliness like a singleton's little black book when I married Dave. He seems to have puttied up a hole in me that had been open too wide for too long. Ours is an old-fashioned type of relationship, our marriage almost like the arranged unions of generations past. Our parents knew each other when they were teenagers. Dave and I met during college, and after years of acquaintanceship and weeks of romance, we knew we would marry. Over five years of marriage we have gotten to know each other, not through long intimate talks (he's a virgin at those) but through life: buying a house together, raising a child with the same values, learning we love nothing better than a night on the couch with books and television, popcorn and ginger ale. Our love has deepened and been enhanced by time, like the color of fine wood that grows richer after years of touch. He takes good care of me. He is my companion, my partner in nearly everything, except now, in this empty hallway where I stand with my new baby. Here I am virtually alone, as I will be on the dark journey to come.

The next morning Dave and Carrie make it to the hospital and help pack up our new possessions: hospital tote bag, ice packs, netted underwear big enough to hold ice packs and giant sanitary pads, pills, baby care booklets, stuffed animals, and boy. We arrive home to find a foil-covered pan on the doorstep, a turkey stew delivered by a neighbor for lunch. We settle the baby in the bouncy seat on the kitchen table, where he will perch until he can sit alone, eat our microwaved food and start planning for his bris. Max will be entered into the covenant of the Jewish people during a ceremony that hasn't mellowed much in its brutality since Abraham first circumcised himself with a sharp rock. It is a rite of passage, which all Jewish boys must endure, that involves inviting all your loved ones over eight days after the birth, hiring a man or woman called a mohel to take a scalpel to the baby's foreskin as he is pinned down by a grandfather on a card table covered with a fine cloth, then serving fish and bagels.

By the time the guests are invited, the food ordered and the mohel and rabbi confirmed, it is night again. I sit on our bed, leaning against pillows, while I nurse Max. It took Carrie five days to learn this skill, but Max got it after a few tries in the hospital. He lies on a pillow on my lap, tummy to Mummy, mouth clamped gently on my chocolate brown areola. They get that dark, I read once, because the contrast of dark nipple to fair skin allows the baby to find nourishment moments after birth, like a neon beer sign guides a drinker to a dark bar. I hold his head in one hand, my breast in another, and a folded towel pressed between the breast he isn't using and the inside of my arm to absorb the leaking milk. It feels so cozy to be on my blue-and-yellow comforter with its Matisse-like flowers and urns, the one I'd bought the previous fall but never used because it was too hot, even in the winter, for my steaming coal-furnace of a pregnant body. I look down at Max's round white cheek, transparent eyelids, and pumping pink lips, then look up at myself in the mirror across the room. I am swollen and pale, matronly in a floral nursing nightgown, but I like what I see: my dream of the past two years come true.

I feel strong and joyful and confident all at once. My black-and-white worldview is exaggerated now, another clue that the PPD is already taking hold. Later, when all the lessons have been learned, I will finally see the world in forgiving tones of gray. But now, all is brilliant white and I truly can't see it ever fading again. I am finally holding the happiness I'd been reaching for during the miscarriages and the tense pregnancy and all the waiting that came before and during. I am home. The baby is alive, healthy, perfect. All the fears and losses are behind us; all the fun and adventure and ease of the future are ahead of us. I can move forward to the life I'd planned for myself, which includes sending Max to day care, resurrecting my wilting writing career, exercising to firmness, buying fashionable clothes after years in soft-fabric sacks, ordering tickets to plays, finding regular babysitters for Saturday nights, planning family vacations to the beach and romantic weekends to the mountains. As soon as Max sleeps through the night, and allows me to get a solid eight hours regularly, it will all start. Three months, tops, I've told myself. All I have to do is get through three more months. I smile at myself, a tired, but satisfied smile. I have made it. It has all worked out.

The happiness is gone the next morning, like a wine buzz metabolized into a hangover. Max is too yellow, we decide, and rush him to the pediatrician. Jaundice is common in nursed babies, but he didn't have it in the hospital, and I need an authority to tell me whether his case is normal. I know a mother whose baby developed cerebral palsy from an untreated case of jaundice that spread to his brain, so I take it seriously. With his deep ocher skin, a clear symptom of jaundice, he looks as if he's spent the month in the islands.

The doctor decides he needs a test for bilirubin, the stuff that shows if the jaundice is serious enough to warrant a sentence under specialized lights or just some time in front of a sunny window. In the basement of the hospital, I force myself to breathe while a technician stabs his tiny purple heel with a needle, then squeezes blood out of the wound into a glass tube as thin as a piece of spaghetti. The results are on the high side of normal, so we must return every other day for blood tests. I worry more about whether he'll be pale enough to have the bris, than about his health. All those people we'd called, all that smoked fish that had to be ordered a week in advance. I drive through the slush and lug his car seat up and down the hallways, my body listing from the weight of it, from the pediatrician's office to the admitting room to the lab until he gets clearance the day before his bris. His tan has faded and a healthy pink is starting to shine through the yellow. Good enough.

I have dreaded the bris for months, can't imagine putting on tights and heels so soon after giving birth, never mind entertaining. I am also not crazy about formal ceremonies. Like many women who develop PPD, I have been punished by high-voltage anxiety since childhood. As a child it manifested itself in my digestive system. I sat in the hallway outside my bedroom crying one morning before school. I was eight years old. I had already missed the bus and my mother was offering to drive me, again, but I refused to go. *I'm going to throw up,* I cried, *I can't go.* I was panicking. I leaned over the white wicker wastebasket in my room and gagged. But I never actually threw up; I only obsessed about it. Usually, I only had stomach cramps and diarrhea so severe that I was sent for a battery of gastrointestinal tests twice during my childhood. I had to drink thick, chalky liquid that later showed up on an X ray as it traveled through my guts. I had to get an enema before the tests so my colon was clear. And always, the tests were negative. The doctors found nothing wrong. Even in children, depression can be invisible.

As I grew, so grew my depression. During sixth grade, I walked through a mall with my friends. I spotted a lonely looking woman leaving the card shop. She had messy gray hair and wore a green tweed coat. She was all alone. Seeing her made me so sad, touched something so deep in me, that I couldn't shake it. I went home and sat on my bed in the late afternoon. The rest of the house was dark. My parents were napping. I wrote in my journal, angry, sad words to try to flush the feelings out of my body. But it didn't work. I was just sad, just so sad, for no reason at all. I couldn't control my erratic emotions, all the melodramatic sorrow and exaggerated terror that plagues those with faulty brain wiring, so I developed habits that gave me a false sense of mastery over my world. Habits such as writing out my angst and drinking and sitting near the doorway in closed rooms. I could tell if something was on my tail, something bad, but if I could keep a step ahead of it, if I could make the feelings it caused go away, I'd be okay. So started my flight from the breakdown that would eventually catch up with me.

As a teenager, I drank entire bottles of cheap white wine to blunt the nervousness, then started smoking pot in my friends' bedrooms. When I was straight, the anxiety bubbled to the surface. I sweated and trembled in the passenger seat of a boy's car on the first date. It was a baby blue BMW and he was a muscle man who I'd invited to my junior prom. He drove me to the beach, a long drive, and I stuck to his seat with perspiration. My mind silently rambled. *Calm down. Breathe deep. You're in control. You can always open the door and jump out. You can open the window if you need to throw up.*

I sat still and breathed shallowly when the door to the math classroom closed. I felt trapped. I always felt trapped. *What if I need to leave? What if I have to go to the bathroom? I'm going to throw up.*

I chose a profession that allowed me to leave whenever I wanted. As a newspaper reporter, I could come and go from the office at will, set up interviews where I felt comfortable, even leave meetings with the excuse that I had to get back to the office to write a story when I got anxious. I learned to hide my anxiety by controlling my environment. Using a lifetime worth of tricks, it sneaks up on me less frequently.

Funerals and weddings are the worst. Anxiety attacks in those situations are a given. I develop a theory about it: I've always been too emotional, I tell myself, and I've learned to tame my overwhelming emotions by stuffing them inside of me. Funerals and weddings are such emotional events and I so fear experiencing strong emotion—it's the ultimate loss of control, after all, for who knows how deep emotions will go before they stop—that the effort of clamping down on these feelings brings on the sweat, rumbling bowels, throbbing heart, faintness, and terror. I always have the urge to run out of the room. I've never left a funeral or wedding before it's over, but I try to sit as close to an exit as possible, just in case. I anticipate the urge to flee striking at my son's bris, and wonder if I will give in to it. I can't leave my own child's bris, can't hide in the bathroom to compose myself.

When the mohel, a white-haired man who looks me in the breasts when he speaks, goes over the ceremony with us in Max's room, the anxiety starts. I pace around the tiny room, keeping busy with the baby, trying to pay attention to what he's telling us about the prayers we will recite. When Dave takes the baby downstairs to wait for the rest of the guests, I rush to the bathroom. I push open that window, rest my chin on the sill, and inhale cold air in slow vibrating breaths until the panic fades. Does this mean the next panic attack will be worse, or that I've gotten it over with? I wonder as I pat my upper lip dry and brush my hair.

I return to the kitchen and sit at the table. I still feel shaken, like a driver after a close call with an eighteen-wheeler. Carrie stands between my legs eating a fat strawberry and I stroke her hair. Liz, a close friend who is always sensitive to my moods, asks how I am. I tell her I'm nervous, and she shields me with her pregnant body from the other people crowding my house.

The mohel, whose name is Sam Pessaroff but is known around the region as *Pecker*off, starts clapping and singing to begin the ceremony. My brother and sister-in-law, Max's godparents, carry Max in on a bed pillow covered with an embroidered linen case. They hand him to his grandmothers, who are visiting for the day. They each kiss one of his cheeks, then give him to Dave's brother, John, who sits with him in a chair that has been designated as the temporary perch for the prophet Elijah. Elijah attends all circumcisions so as to witness the continuity of the Jewish people. Sitting in Elijah's chair with his uncle, Max is blessed by the mohel. Peckeroff then explains the ceremony to the assembled, talking about history and nerve endings that do not register pain at eight days old. He peppers his comments with Borsht Belt humor, relaxing us all, keeping it light. Though he tells the same jokes at every bris, the routine never fails to ease the tension in the room.

"The baby won't be able to have any dates for six weeks, but after that he'll be a well-adjusted Jewish boy, if there is such a thing," he says, as his quick hands remove Max's diaper.

Carrie whines for more strawberries as he talks, until I shove a bagel into her mouth and pick her up. Normally, I would be annoyed that she is disrupting this special moment of her brother's, but I welcome the distraction. I cover my eyes while his penis is cut, then recover to deliver a witty and moving speech about the four Jacobs and one Max he was named for and our wishes that he will be as loved as they were. I only cry once. The mohel says he hopes that all gathered will reunite to see Max stand under the chuppah for his wedding. It is a standard line made all the more poignant when there are those in the room who know they won't live to see the baby's adulthood. One of them is standing across from me. My mother-in-law, Pepper, didn't think she'd live to see Max's birth, and knows she will die before he can speak in sentences. Her eyes fill for the wedding she will not attend, for the boy she will not see grow up, who will never remember her. I look at my husband's mother and weep silently. She is only sixty and I already miss her. Watching her wrestle with cancer has been the family preoccupation for the past year. But this is the first time we see the future without her in it. With tears in our eyes, we sing and clap at the end of the ceremony. Then we feed our guests and absorb well wishes and advice.

After everyone leaves, we collapse with exhaustion. Dave crashes on a chair with his feet up and Carrie lies down with her blanket in front of a video. Max, still drunk from the gauze pad soaked with wine he was given during the bris, sleeps silently in his bouncy seat on the floor. I stretch out on the couch and feel so so tired, as if I've been up for two weeks, which I have. I think of how badly I need to take care of myself and let myself heal, from the pushing and drugs, the stitches and blood loss, the worry and pain. And if I could get that now, if I could have a few weeks to rest and pamper myself like people get after they throw a wedding or put the Christmas tree away, time to decompress, I would be fine. I know I would be just fine. But that's not how it works with babies. With babies, you don't rest until they do.

Chapter 2

Three days after the bris, the sun shines boldly in the sky as it does every March, strong and new, a reminder that warmth, and eventually summer, will return. It is Sunday and the Tupperware containers of meals have stopped arriving. We need food, and the most convenient purveyor is a kosher market one town over.

I lay Max on his blue fleecy snowsuit, zip it around him and tuck the extra fabric from the legs and arms under his body. His skull, still in the malleable state that allowed it to compress while passing from the womb to the world, reminds me of an unpeeled hard-boiled egg. One adult thumb pressed against it too firmly could break right through, I think, as I drape a tiny hat atop it. I strap him into the car seat, which straps into the second seat of the minivan—facing backward for safety, so I can't see whether he's stopped breathing unless I pull the car over and walk around to look. I back the salt-stained red van out of our narrow hill of a driveway, managing not to score the thawing ground with the tires this time. We live in the smallest Colonial in our neighborhood, a twenty-five-year-old subdivision in a bedroom community thirty miles south of Boston. Our town is filled with houses—few historic and beautiful, many new and garish. But besides a popular Chinese restaurant and a few hair salons, there are no real businesses. Most errands take me to the surrounding suburbs. Today, I drive five miles to Cobb's Corner, a collection of stale strip malls that used to be a stagecoach stop, and park in front of the Butcherie.

It is a narrow store with only two aisles. All the local families who keep Kosher, who don't eat cheeseburgers or pork chops or lobster, buy their briskets and fowl, egg noodles and knishes here. We don't observe those traditional Jewish dietary laws, but I've always felt comfortable among this community. Some of the women in long skirts and kerchiefed heads look as though they could be sorting through hunks of crimson meat at a market in nineteenth-century Poland. As I approach, car seat and son swinging from my arm, I am high with pride. I have this beautiful baby and my hardy survivor of a self to show off. Here we are, out and about, ready to take on the world. In my haste to make my debut, I stub my foot on a mound of blackened snow by the curb, lurch forward and nearly pour Max onto the cement sidewalk. Two shoppers who stand outside the door pretend not to notice, but as we pass, they halt their gossip to admire Max. We get the same reception inside. Everyone peers into the car seat, moaning tenderly and placing palms to chests in honor of the sleeping baby. While we wait in line to pay, someone asks his age.

"Eleven days," I announce.

"Eleven days and she takes him to the butcher?" says an elderly woman with a Yiddish accent, shaking her head. "Oy."

Dave and I laugh later as I imitate her old-country inflection, laugh more at her implication that baby and mother should be resting at home like invalids. Later, I will learn, in the most difficult way, that she was right; that mothers and babies do need to be sheltered from the responsibilities of the real world while they recover from a process that splits one body into two.

Other cultures know this well. They see the mother as especially fragile and vulnerable during the postpartum period and practice rituals aimed at protecting and caring for her. There is usually a defined period—often forty days—of rest, seclusion, and help from female relatives, followed by parties to celebrate the woman's new role. Anthropologists who examine these cultures report that there is virtually no postpartum depression in them. They blame our high rates of PPD on our lack of such caring rituals.

Traditionally, Nigerian mothers and babies are cared for by the baby's grandmother in a special hut for two or three months before a feast is held in the mother's honor. Jamaican women, and their babies, are secluded for forty days and cared for by their mothers. The Chinese practice something called Doing the Month. There are two components to this ritual. Zou Yue, sitting the month, involves observing strict rituals. New mothers who observe Zou Yue avoid washing, going outside, eating raw or cold food, being blown by the wind, having sex, reading, being near fans or air conditioners, going to other people's homes, and eating at the table. Women are encouraged to eat a chicken a day during this time. Pei Yue, attending the month, involves being cared for by female relatives for the month. In 1997, Dominic Lee, a researcher at Chinese University of Hong Kong found that 84 percent of women in Hong Kong were still practicing Zuo Yue and 79 percent were taking advantage of the wonderful luxury of Pei Yue. He found that eating chicken, shunning baths, and the other Zou Yue habits had nothing to do with low postpartum depression rates. But those women who were nurtured by mothers, mothers-in-law, or other relatives for more than four hours a day during the first postpartum month had lower levels of PPD than their peers.

But those are distant worlds. The one in which I live expects me to bounce back after birth. It's almost a competition here, to see who can be thin and active, take trips and entertain the soonest after rising from the delivery table. And I don't mind this cultural pressure because I'm anxious to prove I'm up to the challenge.

I won't consider burrowing into bed. After Carrie's birth, I stayed in the house for six weeks. Because of her prematurity the pediatrician had advised against exposing her to crowds. She was born in late November, when it was too cold outside to take her for walks and too crowded with runny-nosed holiday shoppers inside to take her anywhere else. This time I am so excited to get on with life, so anxious to put this pregnancy and all of its restrictions behind me, that I carry on like the proverbial farm wife who returns to harvesting moments after delivering the placenta. If I pretend I'm recovered from pregnancy and childbirth, I reason, then I am. Or I will be sooner. And, really, this last quarter is all that stands in my way.

It's called the fourth trimester, an incongruity that makes perfect sense when you're living through it. The baby might as well not be born yet, for all the humanity it shows. Max is still as communicative as a glove. There are no smiles yet, no focused eye contact, no playing. His greatest achievement is wringing our fingers in his fists.

"Oh, he's squeezing, he's squeezing," guests exclaim, as if they've broken through to a deaf mute. "He's holding my hand. He likes me."

His head flops around like a tassel on top of a winter hat. He sleeps for most of the day. His fiercest cry is still quieter than the squawks from the black crows that announce each morning.

My body is still as far from its prepregnancy state as when it housed Max. Before I heal, I will bleed so profusely for eight weeks that I imagine that one day Dave will come home to find me on the floor, with Carrie howling next to me and a scarlet puddle under my thighs. The flow will taper to normal for a few days, then gush out, because, Dr. Haines explains, it must be pooling somewhere. Though the stitches that repaired my sliced perineum have dissolved, the area between my vulva and anus still feels bruised and swollen. The front of my crotch, where I feared I would unzip, feels raw and tender when I urinate.

Then there is the sleep deprivation. In my opinion, the body feels worse during those first few months of the baby's life than at any time during the pregnancy. Whether you nurse or bottle feed, the baby's cries pull you out of slumber several times a night. Solid nights of sleep are an impossibility for months. And this can easily stomp on even the strongest of mental states. Gary K. Zammit, author of *Good Nights: How to Stop Sleep Deprivation, Overcome Insomnia and Get the Sleep You Need,* writes, "Even a small degree of sleep deprivation can result in depression, anxiety or irritability. If sleep deprivation persists night after night, . . . these emotional and personality changes go on day after day."

I sleep in two-hour stretches, between feedings. Max sleeps next to our bed, on a vinyl-covered pad in a bassinet festooned with chiffon and lace. He's a loud sleeper, snorting and snuffling all night long like his father. Each peep activates the alarm that prepares me to feed, and so many false alarms makes deep sleep rare. Maybe if my brain weren't already starting to melt from the heat of PPD, I would be able to sleep through the baby's snoring. This early, there's no way to tell whether my sleep disturbances are internal or external.

When a real cry sounds, I sit up, pull him onto my lap, unbutton the flap on my nursing nightgown, unlatch the hook on my nighttime bra and feed, like all other female mammals. I curl my spine so my body becomes a lean-to to shelter his, the hair I'd waited so long to grow to one length falling over my face. I flip it over my head, curse it. In April, impatient to shed the excess parts of myself that remind me of how far from normal I am—the heavy, soggy breasts, the marshmallow-squishy belly—I pay someone to cut most of my hair off.

Billy, a flamboyantly gay man who has processed his own receding hair so much that it is now the color of a butternut squash, has been supporting me in my quest for long, feminine hair for months. I once showed him a photo taken of me the night before my wedding, my hair thick and long, the curled ends draping over my tan shoulders, and ever since he's been cheering me on to recapture that fleeting beauty. Now, as I unfold a page from a Victoria's Secret catalog that shows a model with sexy and spunky short hair, he does nothing to dissuade me. I could simply cut bangs again to solve the hair-in-the-face dilemma, or anchor the annoying strands with a barrette. But these solutions never occur to me, nor to Billy, it seems. He just starts chopping away.

He bends down occasionally so that his cheek is next to mine and we are both watching our conversation in the mirror. This way no one can hear when he tells me a tidbit about his lovers.

"He could dress a little better, but undressed he's fine," he says of his current boyfriend.

Usually I'm amused by stories of his dalliances and share some secrets of my own sex life, but today I want to cry. Six-inch sheets of hair the color of oak bark are falling to the floor, revealing more and more of my pale, tired face. *What am I doing?* I think, but say nothing. There is urgency to my action, as if I am punishing someone. It turns out to be myself. With short hair, my ears, pointy chin, and swollen breasts protrude more than ever. The lovely bride-to-be is nowhere to be found.

Rational, I am not. In my old life, if I got to bed too late or had to wake too early I was irritable all day. I felt feverish, moved drunkenly, read sentences of newspaper articles over and over. I am a sleeper, one who needs eight hours a night to function, one who never scheduled a college class before nine A.M., no matter how interesting or pertinent to my degree, one who invented a luscious activity called the Underwear Nap, which involves sleeping in panties and bra, with a partner or alone, in the middle of a weekend afternoon to replenish oneself for the night ahead.

Now, after weeks of being awakened around the clock like a prisoner withholding information, I am beyond cranky and uncomfortable. My thighs ache every morning, never rested from the previous day's lugging of children and their accoutrements. I am aware for the first time in my life of the various parts of my skull—temples, sinuses, cheekbones—because they feel heavy and numb, like nearly frostbitten fingers. No matter what time of day or what I am doing—driving, choosing socks, ordering pizza—I behave as if it is four in the morning and I haven't gone to bed yet.

I dreaded feeling this tired all through my pregnancy. Even without the added burden of PPD, I was pretty miserable about the sleep loss after Carrie was born. But it was the *only* bad thing about her infancy, so I figured if I minimized the sleep deprivation with Max, new motherhood would be a breeze. I set out to do the impossible: control the sleep loss.

Several weeks after I acquaint Max with the butcher, I take him to the pediatrician for a follow-up check of his bilirubin. Ponies gallop away from their merry-go-round on the waiting room wallpaper as I watch Max sleep. "Wake up," I want to yell. "Wake up and you'll be tired at night like the rest of our species." Like most newborns, he sleeps more during the day than the night. In daylight, he can sleep for four hours straight, but not after the sun descends. From all those months of living in the dark, their internal clocks are backwards.

"This one used to sleep all day," a man in the waiting room says, pointing to the baby in his lap. "Then we flipped him."

"Flipped him?"

"My Italian grandmother told me this and I swear it works," he says. "You take the baby and flip 'im, like this, like you're tippin' a football, all the way over and it straightens 'em right out."

"It's true," his wife says, pointing to their baby. "He was so backwards until we flipped him. The next day, he slept all night."

I resist at first, knowing that shuffling a baby's gray matter won't affect his sleep patterns. After a few more days of watching him sleep like a teenager and nights of watching him wake like a baby, I persuade Dave to flip him. He holds Max straight up and turns him over 360 degrees, head over toes, so he ends up in the same position.

"Okay, things will be fine now," I say. "He's sleeping through the night."

And he does sleep that night, for two and a *half* hours before the first feeding.

My next strategy is to join the camp that endorses the family bed as a way to calm the baby with the smell and heat of the mother's body. When he calls for food, I lay him between Dave and me on our king-size bed, roll onto my side so my breast splays like a flattened mound of pizza dough, sculpt his lips on my nipple, and fall back to sleep. If I do this every night, I realize, I won't have to fully wake to feed him or waste any muscle power to sit up or lift him. Two hours later, he cries again. I stuff the first breast back into its harness, roll both of us to the other side of the bed, and offer him his fix. As the milk lets down with the painful tingly sensation of toes being freed from an ice skate, I realize I can't drift off while he nurses on this side because he could fall off the bed. I force myself to stay awake, noticing how furiously my heart beats to accomplish this. I stroke the white fur on his pink ear and rub my fingertip over his terry-cloth jumper to distract myself. He rests serenely, closing his eyes and languidly satisfying his marathoner's thirst. Twenty minutes later, I pull his rag-doll body back to the middle of the bed and sleep, stiff as a veal calf in a pen. I cannot move, cannot spread my arms or roll from front to back because I don't want to crush him. The baby care book that pushes this family slumber party says that's unlikely to happen, but another book, the one that predicts an infant who sleeps with his parents will still be there in fifth grade, hints at SIDS as payment for this convenience. So I concentrate on position while I sleep, which is as restful to me as trying to sleep on a hard slab bunk in a rattling train.

The next morning, I wake to the sound of running water being turned on and off. Dave is shaving. He pulls the razor through the snowfield of foam on his cheek, blasts the water on to rinse the blade, carves another path, rinses again with another loud burst of water. Gray-blue light creeps around the window shades. Max sleeps. I lie flat and count my hours. Though I can't concentrate to read the newspaper, I can remember precisely when I was awakened and for how long. I have a chart in my mind, and if the hours, no matter how broken up, add up to a full night's sleep, I consider myself as rested as everyone else in the world. Eleven to one. That's two. Then one-twenty to three-ten. That's two hours and ten minutes. No, one hour and fifty. Three-thirty to six-fifteen. Two hours and forty-five minutes. Six hours and thirty-five minutes, the slow calculator of my brain registers. That's almost seven. Practically a full night's sleep. I'm fine. The family bed system is working.

It was easier when Carrie was a baby. Though she too woke often to eat, it was always at the same time every night. Max varies his waking times and sleeping durations nightly. After the early morning feeding, I'd fall back to sleep with Carrie until nine or ten. I'd rest when she napped. I sat in the house with her during a wild winter, washing pink hooded towels in baby detergent, jingling musical stuffed animals in front of her eyes, learning to distinguish the voices of the nursery rhyme singing stars. I didn't use much energy for walks or outings until the snow melted, by which time we were all sleeping through the night.

This time, I am up for the day by seven, regardless of Max's nocturnal needs, so I can shower before Dave leaves for work, so I can look presentable when I walk Carrie into her preschool classroom. I am constantly moving, driving her to school, pouring juice and cutting oranges for snacks, fast-forwarding videos through the scary parts while burping the baby, loading grocery bags in and out of the car, exchanging baby gifts, writing ten thank-you notes each day, addressing baby announcement cards, cooking macaroni or hot dogs or eggs for dinner. I am obsessed with keeping our routines and the house in order. Order equals control in my mind. I'm terrified of losing control, so it follows that I can't lose order either. I have maintained a neurotic sense of order all my life. As a little kid, when I went to sleep over at someone's house, I would tame my discomfort at the unfamiliar surroundings by making sure my suitcase was always organized. At my friend Janet's house, I remember leaving the TV room to check on my things. Alone in her room of yellow-checkered walls, I dug my flannel pajamas out of the bag, placed them neatly on top of the other clothes, then refolded and stacked the entire suitcase so it looked freshly packed.

I found my toothbrush and tucked it beside the pajamas. Then I closed the suitcase and placed it squarely beside my pillow. Now, keeping my laundry folded and reducing the unruly stack of baby cards gives me the same false sense of security. Besides, there's no excuse for sloppiness this time. It's one thing for a first-time mother to slack off as she gets accustomed to her new job, I keep telling myself, but not a second-timer. This time, it is not a restful fourth trimester, not a time for settling into the job. But it will only last three months, I remind myself daily, just get through three months.

The one item I didn't have during Carrie's infancy, and which I know will free me from exhaustion more successfully than trying to manipulate Max's sleep, is an electric breast pump. When he is old enough to take a bottle without forgetting the more difficult skill of operating my nipples, I pack Max into the car and drive up the highway to a stucco Victorian that serves as headquarters for Lactation Care, Inc. A fiftyish woman with a straight pageboy haircut and no noticeable breasts of her own explains and demonstrates how the electric pump works. She presses plastic cups to her sweater in the same places where my enormous glands protrude and assures me I'll be able to drain two at once in no time.

"Just read the pamphlet," she says. "And call us if you have any questions."

She takes my credit card and embosses it on a machine in the kitchen while I wait at the dining room table. I had hoped for a little TLC from this woman, strokes to my head, herbal tea, an offer to watch the baby while I sleep for twelve hours. But she seems anxious to get me out of there, so I bundle Max into his snowsuit and car seat as quickly as I can. The woman offers to carry him to the minivan while I lug the case that holds the pump in one hand and the paperwork in the other. I balance the strap of a plum-colored diaper bag on one shoulder and a bulging pocketbook on the other, and clamp a set of keys that hang from a brass Minnie Mouse chain between my elbow and ribs. My hands and arms are always full these days; if I were to trip on the jagged cement path leading to the street, I couldn't break my fall with my palms if I wanted to.

The van sits at the curb, its side door wide open, one tire on the sidewalk.

"Oh, look, I forgot to close to the door," I say, trying to sound amused. "I guess I'm a little tired."

She smiles and hands me my son.

"You want to pull this over his chest so it's nice and snug," she says, adjusting a strap on his car seat and making me feel neglectful and stupid. "Bye now."

She rushes up the porch steps and back to her business. I rush home to examine my new toy. The pump will smooth out the whole sleeping and feeding system by allowing me to collect a bottle of milk each morning that Dave can feed the baby each night before he goes to bed. This means I will be able to get a four-hour stretch of sleep, as long as I get to bed by nine.

The next morning, an hour after I nurse Max and an hour before he needs to nurse again, I plug in the pump. Clear plastic tubes connect to the cups, which screw into the bottles. With one hand, I hold a cup and bottle over each nipple. With the other, I set the power dial to three, the speed to medium, and the switch to on. A pump on top of the machine starts pulsating in steady, even strokes, like a mechanical bull bucking up and down in graceful rhythm. The air pulls at the cups, which stretch my nipples straight out until they start releasing milk. It works! After ten minutes of milking, one bottle holds two ounces, the other three, plenty for one feeding. I shut off the pump, break the suction between the cups and my skin, pour the liquid gold into disposable bottles, and wash all the parts, including my own breasts, sticky with dried sweet milk.

When Max is two months old, I plan to take advantage of my newfound freedom at a family wedding. I have looked forward to this cousin's nuptials for months. It is to be my debut: dressed up, without child, ready to lean against my husband on the dance floor like other grown-ups. As long as I pump at the right time during the wedding, and get home before the breast milk I've left for Max runs out, everything will be great. Not only will I have a fun night, but I'll leave with a bottle of milk in my portable cooler, sort of a party favor just for me. That could buy me another few hours away from the baby.

Dave cuts in front of a waiter carrying a tray of stuffed mushrooms as he rushes to hand off the pump to me. The reception, a late-afternoon affair at a country club, has begun. We've just come in from the edge of the golf course where the ceremony took place amid gales of cold wind and ashen clouds. I grab two mushrooms to quell the ferocious hunger that's built up since I began pumping. Burning an extra 500 calories a day when I feed Max makes me famished enough; vacuuming milk out of myself when I don't need to feed the baby compounds the hollow bones feeling.

"We'll be in the ladies room," I tell him, taking the pump and a bag of bottles and towels. "Save me some food."

My mother follows me, to keep watch. The ladies room doesn't have any seats, so we head for the members' locker room. There are plenty of wooden benches between the lockers, but few electrical outlets.

"Here's one," Mom says, crouching near the floor. She seems excited about the adventure.

I plug in and set up the pump, straddle the bench, and pull my dress down to my waist. It is a hot-pink sleeveless crepe number that I bought at a bargain warehouse. I didn't want to waste money on something that wouldn't fit once my boobs deflate, and it shows. I usually wear elegant dresses to weddings. My closet consists primarily of Levi's jeans, T-shirts, and chic black dresses that I've only worn once. But this time covering the thick bra straps and disguising the lumpiness of the leak shields in the cups was my goal.

"I think I hear someone. Go check."

I'm worried that a golfer will witness this bizarre scene and start screaming at me while I'm topless.

"There's no one there. Just relax," my mother says, uncharacteristically calm herself. She tends to be nervous about details in strange situations, but her job as lookout woman seems to have inspired confidence. Or maybe everyone seems placid compared to me.

We talk about the wind, the bride's dress, and the resemblance of various relatives until I flick the machine off and prepare to pack seven ounces of milk into the soft-sided cooler I bring everywhere.

"Can you get the insulated thing out. It's in the bag."

"I don't see it," she says.

"Let me look. Hold the milk. Carefully."

She's right. I've forgotten the cooler and freezer pack that will preserve the milk until I get home. I pour it down the sink, the watery white liquid dulling the sheen on the brass drain cover. All those nutrients, meant to plump up Max's brain cells and fortify his immune system, go instead to a sewage pipe. I shove fresh paper shields into my bra and return to the reception. So much for another outing.

Dave and I sit with his cousins, a handsome group that spends the night trying to one-up each other with put-downs. No one talks to me; not the stunning girlfriend in the pale satin dress or the elegant wife in diamonds. I don't talk to them either; I have no interest in their uncomplicated and restful lives. I'm not usually this bitter, but I blame it on the lack of sleep. A friend of mine, a rabbi's wife with a small baby of her own, tells me I should forgive anything I think or do while this sleep-deprived.

"They used sleep deprivation to torture people in concentration camps, you know," Becky says. "Give yourself a break."

My breasts are starting to fill again, like gutters collecting rainwater, and I can't bear to lose another feeding. I've got to get home so Max can drain them.

"Do you mind if we leave soon?" I ask Dave before dessert.

"Do you want to dance first?"

"I can't."

The next morning Dave pours himself a cup of coffee.

"Is there enough for me?" I ask.

"No. Do you want me to make more?"

"I'll do it. You change him," I say, handing him a baby weighed down by a saturated diaper.

I'm normally a decaf tea drinker. I am so sensitive to caffeine that I developed withdrawal headaches when I gave up my one cup of real tea a day because I was too anxious in the morning. But I'm taking care of two kids on broken sleep and I need a drug. An upper. Caffeine is the only legal one in our kitchen. It is yet another tool I can use to control my fatigue.

I pack away my Twinnings English Breakfast and forage into Dave's sack of Eight O'Clock beans. I collect four scoops of grounds, which look like the rich earth of deep trenches, and sprinkle a layer of cinnamon over them before turning the coffee machine on. The result, strong and hot, mellowed by milk and sugar, is as seductive as a chocolate dessert. I pour deep mugs of it, savor them all morning. The fog in my temples starts to clear and power returns to my bones. It is the opposite of what happens when a soothing bath of alcohol courses through the body. I can almost feel the energy flowing through my veins and awakening every cell, like electricity, like the fairy godmother's wand tapping me on the head and sending a wave of glowing magic through me.

From that day on, I belong in America, not England, where coffee rules and tea is for wimps. Once I'm sure the caffeine isn't affecting Max's sleep—he's still crashed most of the day, no matter what he sucks through my breast milk—it becomes a regular part of my diet. My battery usually stays charged all day, and when it falters earlier, I pull up to a fast-food window and order a large Coke. I am truly addicted. I need and love my drug with equal zeal. I coo to Dave at night about the wonders of coffee, and how foolish I was not to convert sooner. It is a miracle elixir, getting me through the sleepless days. Often, I don't even feel tired. Like an alcoholic who drinks to squelch emotions, I use caffeine to deny my exhaustion.

And I certainly get a lot accomplished. As the snowbound crocuses of early spring give way to vibrant buds and grasses that delight botanist and allergist alike, I start to venture out more. I go out alone at night for the first time to a meeting at Carrie's school. I chat with every parent I know and sit next to a woman I've wanted to get to know. She wears an ankle bracelet and colored jeans and once complimented me on an essay I wrote for the local paper. We talk about infertility and sex and husbands, and when I get home I am flying with excitement. A night out! Fun! Adult conversation!

I am still wired when I wake to nurse Max. A continuous loop of the evening plays in my head. "I got to sit next to her. She's my new friend. I have a new friend. She wears an ankle bracelet. She's my friend."

Suddenly, I realize I have to reach out to more people so I can have more great experiences like this. I plan to invite the mothers of all Carrie's school friends over for lunch. An end of school party. I'll make tuna. As I nurse, I go through all the foods and dishes I'll set on the table as if I'm flipping through a catalog. I see my glass bowls, apple-shaped salt shaker, floral cloth napkins float before my eyes. After I rest Max on my shoulder to let the milk settle into his belly and tuck him under a thermal blanket in his crib, I watch every detail of the meeting, the conversation, the luncheon in my mind. I eventually get sick of the tape and hungry for sleep, but I can't shut it off. This is a classic PPD symptom, the brain spinning like a hamster's wheel.

I keep watching the clock as I try to clear the screen in my mind. Minutes, then chunks of hours, pass. I panic. I can't be this tired. It's bad enough getting up for twenty minutes three times a night. I can't waste more time. I need to take care of the kids. I'm in charge. If I don't get to sleep now, I think, I could lose them. As it is, I feel like a refugee carrying my children down a long dirt road, terrified that any minute I will collapse and drop them and someone else will have to take care of them and no will ever trust me with them again. Nothing makes sense. Every fear is exaggerated, every thought brings alarm. Two hours after my mind starts to abuse itself, I fall asleep.

I feel much better the next morning, and I'm hyper again the day of the luncheon. While Carrie is at school, I clean the basement playroom, wipe the dog's paw prints off the sliding glass door, wash the kitchen floor, dust the surface of every vase and picture frame and candlestick, make tuna salad and green salad and fruit salad, brew iced tea, set the dining room table for adults and the kitchen table for kids, and buy bread and dessert. Then I pick her up and lead the guests back to our house.

"I don't know how you can do this with a newborn," Ann says. "I couldn't do it with two older kids."

"Well, look at him," Linda says, pointing to Max, asleep in his car seat. "He's so good. He just sleeps."

I bustle about serving and clearing while they discuss school buses and teachers. The kids run by with peacock feathers my daughter collected at a friend's farm.

"Put that down, Jason," Ellen says. "I don't let him play with those things. They're gross. They could have diseases."

I don't say anything, about how much fun feathers are and how unlikely it would be for salmonella to live on a feather for this long and how rude she is to imply that my kid's things aren't good enough for her kid and how bad the chunks of maroon highlights in her dyed black hair look. I just watch the clock and wait for them to leave. I want them to shut up. I can't stand hearing voices anymore. It hurts my head to pay attention for this long. I am easily overstimulated, another typical PPD symptom. And I'm weary. I couldn't fall asleep for an hour after Max nursed the night before.

I mention the bouts of insomnia to Dr. Haines at my postdelivery check-up.

"How much are you sleeping every night?"

I tell her the good news: I'm getting four hours at a time while Dave feeds Max the bottle.

"I'd like to see you getting more five and six hour stretches," she says, as she presses my shrunken uterus.

"How do I do that?" I say, not bothering to hide my aggravation. She should be proud of me. How does she expect me to do better than this? Does she have a magic formula for forcing babies to sleep through the night?

"Have your husband get up at night," she answers. "Do what you have to do. I don't want you to get depressed."

She will later tell me that she gives this warning to new mothers who are getting little sleep and who have some other stressor in their lives at the time of the six-week appointment. I don't know what stress she sees, but she does not know about my history of depression. I never tell people, even doctors. When filling out a form that asks if I've ever been depressed or had counseling, I always lie, as if denying it will make it unreal.

"Sleep deprivation can increase your sensitivity to depression," she will explain later. "You have no reserves left."

She is right, of course, to advise me to get more sleep. But I am in no shape to hear it. I drive across the street to the mall after the appointment, still annoyed at her hyperbole. *Depressed!* I'm not unhappy at all, just tired. How dare she scare me by throwing that word into the conversation. I'm not depressed. I'm not one of those depressed mothers I've read about in articles in the *Boston Parents' Paper*. I'm a perfectly capable mother. I'm just tired. So tired, in fact, that I decide to take advantage of my solitude. I park the car and climb into the backseat. Behind the tinted windows no one can see me close my eyes for a few minutes of rest. At the time I don't even see how bizarre this is.

Sleep doesn't come here, either, so I head into the department store. I need a new dress—an attractive one this time—for a graduation party next month.

Our friend Mike has rented out an Italian restaurant in Providence to celebrate his wife Andrea's master's degree. Dave will meet me after work and the kids will stay at my parents' house. Later, I'll return there to sleep and Dave will drive to our house alone so he can get to work the next morning.

There is rich food and expensive wine and an insurance saleswoman pushing her wares across the table from me. It is late June and I walk up the city streets to my car after the dinner wearing nothing but a sleeveless dress. I leave at precisely eleven so I can get home to sleep. It is normally a fifteen-minute drive back to my parents' house and I look forward to buzzing down the empty highway. But as soon as I pick up speed, I see red taillights ahead. Everyone is stopped. Every car I see on the hill up ahead is idling. The blinding lights of a road construction crew glow from miles ahead. I roll down the window and let the night air stroke my face. It is warm and windy and navy blue. Aerosmith howls on the radio and I turn it up, reminded, with my head out the window, of the summer nights I spent in Newport before marriage and babies and curfews imposed by the body. We barhopped in miniskirts and deep tans. We danced in the street to a jazz band on a night that felt like noon in August. We kissed strange men under streetlights, then met for french fries to tell the tales.

And now, ten years later, tears fill my eyes. Not for those days, so much, but for this one. I think I might fall asleep in the car. I won't get enough sleep if this traffic doesn't start moving. I have a baby to feed. I have a kid to take care of tomorrow. Max is three months old. He should be sleeping through the night by now, but he's not. The fourth trimester is over. Life should be completely back to normal. But it has deviated much further from normal than I realize. I wake almost every hour, every time a sound leaves his nose. I lift him out of bed and pull him to my breast. Even when Dave feeds him the bottle and thinks I am sleeping, I run down the stairs.

"Why are you here?" he asks.

"He's crying," I say. "I can't stand the crying."

"He wasn't crying. He's just lying here drinking."

But I hear him cry. All night. All day. Over the rumble of the jackhammer cutting up the highway.

Chapter 3

The mind of a person heading into serious clinical depression is like a radio in a car driving through the mountains. The clear connection to the music either fades slowly or cuts in and out as the trip progresses. But there is always one moment when it is obvious that the connection has broken and there is nothing to hear but static. For me, that moment came on the day the nanny visited.

If there were a diagnostic test, some kind of MRI, that could detect the evaporation of the last drop of seratonin lubricating my brain, it would have identified it on that day. Like someone who can trace her back problems to a specific day when she lifted a particularly heavy item, I can trace my descent into irrationality to a still morning when I stand by Max's crib and believe that Wendy Stephens, a professional nanny, will be replacing me. I have only hired Wendy for one day a week, but I might as well be sending Max to boarding school for all the angst it causes. It is true that paying someone to do a job I've done by myself until now means that I'm letting go of my role as full-time mother. But it feels bigger than that. Every emotion, every high and low, is exaggerated these days, as if some knob that controls perspective has rusted away. In my corroded mind, I am not only changing my job description; I am subletting my baby. For months, while I unravel then start to knit myself back together, I will blame the stress of Wendy's visit for my breakdown. Then I will realize that even if I hadn't faced separation from Max, even if I had never met Wendy, I would have broken anyway. But on this day, when the months of exhaustion and the continuing disintegration of my brain chemicals finally do me in, Wendy assumes the role of final straw.

It is one of those sunny days that bruise the eyes, when looking into the backyard causes one's pupils to dilate so abruptly that it feels as if a muscle has been yanked inside the skull. In the winter in New England, when the sun reflects off the snow and the same thing happens to the eyes, it's a pleasant reminder that the sun still exists. But it's startling in the summer, when brightness isn't supposed to hurt. Today is Max's four-month birthday, and Wendy has come to meet him. I have already interviewed Wendy by myself and decided to hire her if Max seems comfortable with her. Starting next month, she will watch him every Friday while I rebuild my atrophied writing career and edit a newsletter. On Mondays and Wednesdays he will spend the day with six other kids at the home of one of the best day-care workers in town. Marge Drake, a mother of four grown children and a day-care provider for twenty years, has a bright, clean playroom built onto the side of her house; swings, slides, sandboxes, and a climbable wooden train engine in the yard, and an assistant to help daily. I'd first called Marge while I was still pregnant to see if she anticipated any openings for the fall. She'd said no, but called me when Max was only a few weeks old to tell me she had an unexpected opening for September. If I wanted it, I had to let her know that week. The idea of turning my newborn over to a stranger seemed impossible then, but I trusted the friends who had trusted her with their babies, and I didn't want to pass up the opportunity. Besides, I expected the tension to ease as the time got nearer. Probably, I reasoned, I would be ready for a break by then. Maybe I would even be tired of tending to Max by myself. Neither has happened yet, and whenever I think about the day I will hand him over to Marge, my stomach hurts. Nevertheless, my anxiety about day care is still at a manageable level. It's still too far away to seem real yet. Wendy, who will take care of him only on Fridays and is sitting across from me in my dining room chair, is very real.

I can't stop staring at her necklace. Hanging from the throat of the thirty-four-year-old is a solid-gold man hoisting a barbell over his head. It is a violent little trinket, threatening and intimidating in its blatant display of power. But everything else about Wendy is gentle. In her Jamaican lilt, which reminds me of palm tree vacations and sifting marijuana seeds in record album covers, she tells of her extensive experience. She's served as live-in nanny for twin preschoolers since they were born, and only wants to leave that job so she can live elsewhere with her new husband. She jokes with Carrie about the mix-ups that will occur when she works for us because our dog is also named Wendy. She brushes a brown finger across Max's cheek, and he smiles in response.

"Let me show you Max's room," I say.

I carry Max up the stairs and Wendy follows. When we reach the doorway of the tiny rectangular room, where gray hippopotami wearing blue-and-pink striped rugby shirts dance along the wallpaper, I ask if she wants to hold him.

"You know how to hold babies, right?" I ask, as I hand him over.

"Oh, yes. I know babies," she says, something in her tone inviting further inquiry.

"Do you have any of your own?"

"Yes. Yes. I have a daughter, twelve. She lives with her grandmother."

"In Jamaica?"

She nods.

"Will she come here to live with you?"

"Oh, yes. She'll come this summer. For two weeks."

I know Wendy has lived in this country for five years. That means she left her own child at age seven. Though it is common for women in her culture to do this, out of economic necessity, it makes me question her values. What kind of mother does that? How could I let such a woman take care of my baby? What kind of mother does that make *me?*

I had already decided to send Max out to be tended to, like dry-cleaning, while I was pregnant with him. Though I'd traded a full-time newspaper reporter's job for the spotty work of a freelance writer before getting married, I never intended to stop writing completely. The freelancing continued while Carrie was a baby, but the older she got the less I wrote. I didn't have time to hustle for new assignments, or come into contact with many people or events worth chronicling. Over the years, as Carrie's brain sparked with new experiences, mine shriveled. Like a houseplant that only gets sun on one side, I grew lopsided. All my energy, all my growth, went to the art of mothering with none leftover for writing. Still, I couldn't bring myself to send Carrie to day care. Initially, I was too attached to her, and too afraid that I would lose her if I let someone else care for her, either to an accident or because she would suffer irreparable psychological damage from being watched by neglectful strangers. By the time I realized she'd be fine in other hands, she was a three-year-old who didn't like change or being away from me for long periods of time. It seemed cruel to make her adjust to a separation just so I could be happy.

But I did acknowledge that I wasn't happy as a full-time mother. The therapist I saw while I was pregnant with Max helped me to realize that I wanted more as I raised this second child. I'd gone to her initially because I was terrified of having an anxiety attack during my mother-in-law Pepper's inevitable funeral, and running out of the chapel. Dave would need me then, for once, and I didn't want to let him down when my role would be to sit tall and hold his hand. I also didn't want to pull such a social faux pas in front of Pepper's friends and relatives. They all appear to fulfill their roles so flawlessly, just like she does. The thought of ruining the decorum of her funeral with my anxiety problems still horrifies me. I imagine the talk: "the daughter-in-law fled the chapel, leaving her grieving husband behind!" After all Pepper's bragging about what a great find I was, they would all see me for the failure I think I am.

The therapist, an intelligent woman with long hair on her head and unshaved legs, talked with me about the funeral. But mostly we discussed my general sense of discontent. She suggested, as most of my therapists have, that I commit to some extensive therapy. But I didn't think that was necessary. In my rulebook for keeping depression at bay, short-term therapy with a social worker to work on a specific problem has always been okay, although I'm ashamed every time I add a new therapist to my list. Analyses or visits to a psychiatrist are unacceptable. Those are for sick people, the truly mentally ill. Going to a shrink would mean I need one; that I have lost the race and mental illness has out-ranked me. Going to a social worker just means I'm having a few problems adjusting. So after several months, I left her office, happy with the decision that I would be a working mom.

Max couldn't miss a twenty-four-hour mom if he never had one. If I worked part-time, I decided, and had others watch him part-time, he could grow up knowing me as a content working woman instead of a resentful mommy. We could both be happy. And now it is all in place, scheduled to begin in September, when he is six months old. That is when my life will start again, with time to write and run for miles and feed sun to the wilted parts of me.

I should be happy that the plans are finalized, and relieved that both kids like Wendy and that she has made them laugh. But there is a different feeling in me, or lack of feeling, where excitement and anticipation belong. I am both numb and stunned, like someone who's been scared to death by a strange sound late at night. What I don't realize is that leaving a child in the hands of others "ranks right up there as one of the most traumatic adaptations of new motherhood," according to Kleiman and Raskin, authors of *This Isn't What I Expected: Overcoming Postpartum Depression.* Other PPD authorities advise against making major life changes during the postpartum period because they add stress to an already stressful situation. And that can only push a woman heading toward PPD closer to the breaking point.

After Wendy leaves, I bring Max back upstairs for his nap. I put him down among the soft blue and green blankets and feel something break inside me. A complete stranger is going to put my baby down for his nap. A stranger—a woman who abandons her own child—will be the last face he sees before drifting off to sleep. If he's scared or hurt, I will be gone. A complete stranger will have control of my baby.

A complete stranger will have control of my baby.

I have held on for a long time, through two difficult years since I decided to have a second child. There were two miscarriages, treatment for infertility, nights spent in intensive care units watching my mother-in-law fight her demon cells, a pregnancy plagued with fears of failure, preterm labor, and these four months of burning all my energy without replenishing any. I have held on so tightly for so long that I've forgotten I'm doing it. I have never let my smile fade, never cried that it was too much to take, watching the kids all day and hoisting all the groceries into the car on so little sleep. I have never given up and run away, or left Dave with a refrigerator full of bottles while I spent just one day in bed, with furniture blocking the bedroom door so none of them could peck bits of flesh out of me. I have never done any of those mentally healthy things, those acts of surrender that allow one to recharge. I can't. If I let go, the depression that's been hovering around me all my life might just land. I've simply held on for much too long, like the weightlifter on Wendy's necklace trying to show off how strong he is. I am about to let go completely. When I look back from the safety of recovery, I will see that in that one morning, I lost any grip I had on myself.

I just don't realize that yet.

.   .   .

What kind of mother am I?

It's a common question that PPD sufferers ask themselves. We are famous for judging ourselves as horrible mothers, probably because self-criticism and feelings of inadequacy are two of the more popular emotional symptoms of the disease. The question blasts through my head so often the afternoon of Wendy's visit that it seems to preface all other thoughts. It's not just the prospect of child care that brings on the doubts; there is also the reality of Max's scaly face. He has patches of eczema the color of maraschino cherries on both of his whipped-cream-white cheeks. Though I've worried about the rashes being an indication of food allergies, I haven't read anything about eczema until today. I suspect the rash is a signal that I shouldn't wean him when he's six months old so others can care for him, and that I shouldn't be feeding him baby food and formula now in the hopes that a full stomach will inspire him to sleep through the night. But I haven't wanted to see it in print. Now I read over and over and over again in *What to Expect the First Year* two sentences that confirm my fears. "Approximately one in three children with eczema will develop asthma or other allergies later. Breastfeeding, particularly when there is a family history of allergies, for at least six months, preferably for a year may help."

Dave, his father, has asthma and allergies. Sometimes at night I wake to the sound of a thousand voices clamoring wildly, a distant crowd yelling in unison. Then I realize the world outside my window is silent and the sound comes from inside my husband's chest as his asthmatic lungs struggle to collect air. I once fed Dave a spoonful of ice cream that had almonds in it, not knowing he was allergic to them. His mouth began to itch and he spit the ice cream into a sink before his throat could swell, which could have suffocated him. My beloved cat, Simon, cannot even come into our bedroom anymore because his lush orange fur inflames Dave's lungs so. Almonds and fish, cat fur and springtime, these are the dangers to an asthmatic with allergies. Max may have inherited the same weaknesses. By not breastfeeding for a year, or two, or until Max can unhook my bra himself, I am subjecting him to these dangers. But I have no intention of breastfeeding one day beyond Max's six-month birthday. After that I will be focusing on myself, with small firm breasts and a head full of story ideas. I don't even want to nurse him exclusively for six months. I need to start weaning if I'm going to be emancipated in September. And he needs to eat strained pears and drink stick-to-the-ribs formula so he'll start sleeping. I need to do it for me, even though there is a good chance he will suffer for the rest of his life if he's carrying his father's blueprint for a hypersensitive immune system.

What kind of mother am I?
I flip between the pages on eczema, asthma, and food allergies, hoping that reading them enough times will reveal a loophole that will free me from my guilt. I am sitting beneath a short birch tree on the shore of a cloudy disk of water. We have come to this beach, strewn with cigarette butts and goose droppings, to celebrate the Fourth of July with our fellow townsfolk. It is an annual tradition, involving unwinable games of chance and rides that fold up like card tables at the end of the night. Local organizations such as a group that raises money to spay and neuter stray cats, and a temple brotherhood comprised of former fraternity boys, peddle hot dogs and dewy cans of soda.

We had hoped to run into friends here, but no one we know has arrived yet. Dave stands at the edge of the water where Carrie fills and empties buckets of muddy sand. Max sleeps in his stroller. At nightfall, fireworks like flying gemstones will illuminate the water that reflects them.

I can't wait for the fireworks to start or to end. I wish everything away these days, never enjoying the present, desperate to get somewhere else, somewhere more comfortable. So when the fire bursts in the sky at exactly nine-thirty and the adults and children pressed all around me ooh and ahh, I can think of nothing but bed. It's getting late. I look behind us, instead of up into space, and try to map out the fastest route to the car. We have to go, I think, this is too loud for the kids. I look at Carrie, with her hands over her ears and an astonished look on her face, and I hope she will cry. As a child, I always cried at fireworks, until my mother ran with me to the safety of a quiet car for the rest of the show. If my daughter cries now, I will have to offer her the same protection. We will have to leave.

Finally, before the most beautiful explosions overlap in the sky at the end, I tell Dave we should leave so we don't get stuck in traffic. We live only half a mile away, but still, hundreds of cars could clog the only road to our neighborhood if we don't get a head start. He hates traffic, so he doesn't argue. I push the double stroller on its rickety plastic wheels over tree branches and through sand traps as quickly as possible, riding over blankets and blocking views. I have to get to bed, where I can lie and wait until morning so I can wish that away, too.

At a few minutes past two the next morning, I wake up startled, though the house is silent. I check on Max, who sleeps peacefully with his bottom pointed to the ceiling. He only wakes once a night now, which brings my insomnia into clear focus. Getting up to feed him every two hours masked it, but now that I am the only one awake, it is obvious the problem is mine. I wish he would wake more often, so I could hide behind his needs again.

I then wander into Carrie's room, where there is always a lamp on. I slide onto her single bed, cuddling next to her and lay my head on a small corner of her pillow. Her room is big and airy, with pale pink walls, calico curtains tied with satin ribbons, and framed prints of pages from children's literature on each wall. The Goodnight Moon bunny crawls under his covers, drowsy and ready to sleep. The Runaway Bunny's mother pulls him close and tells him he can never run away from her love. Peter Rabbit's mother makes chamomile tea to sooth his stomach while he sleeps his adventures away. Carrie's comforter is soft and pink, and her body, sleeping, is as reassuring as the arms of a parent at the approach of a stranger. She asks nothing of me, just gives soft steady breaths that would be as pink as her walls if air had color.

Later, when I am well, I will still feel soothed in her presence. I will come to believe that it is a chemical thing, that she, like my husband, is composed of an arrangement of elements that when exposed to mine create calm. Call it yin and yang, opposites attracting, any number of clichés, but the presence of Carrie and Dave bring me peace. Max, who is more like me in personality and, probably in chemistry, churns me up in a way that is both exhilarating and draining. These insights come later, in the calm of sanity. But on this night, as I lay beside my daughter, I simply feel safe, like a child who has crawled into her mother's bed. My muscles soften and sleep comes easily.

But only for a short time, for when I wake I am bathed in remorse. I had a friend whose mother slept with her every night instead of with the husband she loathed. This inappropriate ritual had stolen my friend's innocence, delivered the message that if she was providing safety for her mother, there was certainly no safe place for her. She became the grown-up, losing more and more of her childhood every night her mother stretched her rough legs under the sheet. I always hated that mother, who was so obviously disturbed. And now I have become her—the crazy lady who takes comfort from a three-year-old. Though there is nothing sexual about my visits to Carrie's bed, I am still aware that this role reversal is inappropriate. While Carrie sleeps, I use her like a security blanket, depend on her to get through part of the night. No one knows, not Carrie nor Dave. Just I, as I return, feeling creepy and

deranged, to my own bed. I have done it before, during these
months when I am despondent with insomnia, and I will do it again
before I recover, but never without the guilt.

After I nurse Max in the morning I lay him next to me in
my bed and he falls immediately back to sleep. As I watch him, my
chest feels as though it has split open, fresh sorrow bursting
through like tulip buds breaking brittle spring soil. This, too, has
happened on other mornings and will happen again. Good-bye, I
say to him in my mind, I am so sorry to leave you. I don't know
where I am going or when it will happen, but I have a feeling that I
will leave him soon. This must be what it feels like when you know
you're dying, and you look at your loved ones with longing and regret all the time. A vision of water going down a drain drags past
my open eyes. I see Max lying here alone, a tiny pastel body among
yards of rumpled white sheets. I feel I must apologize in advance for
abandoning him. He needs me, but I am slipping, slipping down
that drain. I know this makes no sense. This feeling, as if I am pre-
dicting my death, terrifies me. I try to figure it out. Where am I going? Why do I feel this way? But the answers don't come, just a kind
of mourning, for whatever great thing I am about to lose.

The Monday after the Fourth of July weekend, I have a reason
to escape the scary morning mind tricks. It is Carrie's first day
of camp. I must get up early to make sure her bag is packed with a
towel and an extra set of clothes, labeled in indelible ink *Carrie R.*
Carrier, it looks like. She needs to eat breakfast quickly so I can
dress her in a bathing suit and smooth thick white sunscreen into
her pale skin. I'll also have to dress Max, feed him, and pack a diaper bag with Cheerios and rattles.

Carrie goes to camp at the same place she went to nursery
school, except many of the kids and teachers are different in the
summer. Every day during the school year I have handed her off to
the same teachers, stopped on the sidewalk outside the building

to talk to the same mothers. Now, I smile at strangers as we walk into the school together. It is disorienting, being in a familiar place with unfamiliar people. I suddenly feel unsafe. Caught without the armor I would normally wear into a new situation, I curl my fingers into my palms.

"Bye-bye, Sweetie," I say, as I kneel on the rug to hold Carrie. "I'll be back after lunch to get you. Have a great time."

"I will, Mama," she says, looking over my shoulder at the kids coming in.

"And remember: Mommy always comes back."

I have said this to her since she started school, my refrain to remind her that she is not being abandoned. I've always assumed that a child's separation anxiety stems from the fear that her mother will never return, that she'll forget or get sick before they reunite. For Carrie the slogan, *Mommy always comes back,* has either successfully quelled such fears or wasn't necessary in the first place. She's always adjusted flawlessly to separation, as long as she knows it will end soon. She never cries when I leave, not on her first day of school and not today.

But I want to cry. I walk up the stairs that lead outside and that feeling, of homesickness and going down the drain, washes over me again. I am alone with Max for the first time in six weeks. In the gap between the end of school in May and the beginning of camp in July, other mothers have shopped for children's bathing suits, passed the days handing out juice boxes and dusty orange crackers at the lake, and complained about the unstructured days. I've spent the time shadowing my daughter for security. That same sense of peace I absorb in her bed also grounds me during the day. And there is another element. With Carrie, I have always felt competent as a mother. So, like an algebraic equation, if it has been proven that I am a competent mother with Carrie, then with Carrie by my side, I am still a competent mother. With her to anchor me, I know I can get through the days. I have done it before, perfectly, so I know I can do it again. But without her, I come unglued. I don't want to be alone with Max. He is beautiful, and smiles at everyone, and rarely fusses, but he scares me. It is an old sensation of fear, one I haven't felt since I was six years old. My mother lets go of my hand by the edge of the YMCA pool before my swimming lesson and walks out of sight. Terror and panic consume me. I cry and cry while the instructors pull me across the pool, metallic-tasting water soaking my tongue when my chin sinks below the surface. I am alone and in danger. That was how I felt then. That is how I feel today.

I only have three hours until I pick up Carrie, three hours alone with Max. Keeping busy will make the time go faster. I drive to a dingy mall near our house. By the time I get there, he is asleep in his car seat. I don't want to wake him by snapping it out of the car, and I don't have to yet because the stores aren't even open. I shut off the engine, then turn the key to the farthest notch so the radio plays. A song by the 10,000 Maniacs, a rock band lead by a singer with a voice that sounds as if it's made of velvet and crystal, has just started. The sky is coal gray, she sings, her mood is darker and she can't get out of bed. Sad words sung to cheery, foot-tapping music. I love this song. It always reminds me of my friend Tom, a smart, handsome guy I worked with as a reporter. He read thick books of literature and taught me to make curried chicken. He moved to Maine to build wooden boats and ended up cutting off a finger. I moved to New Jersey and got engaged. He called me when he got married and promised that he and his wife would call whenever they were in Boston, which was often, but he never did. I called to harass him about drifting out of touch. He told me he was expecting a baby and would send an announcement as soon as it arrived. I decided not to be the one to call first again because the friendship was starting to feel too one-sided. He still hasn't called.

I've missed him before, wished he would call me to talk, wished that thing that happens to men when they marry, that makes them not need their women friends anymore, hadn't happened. But this morning, as Max sleeps behind me, the longing sears me. I miss Tom as if he were a child I've lost. Tears, like the ones I shed into the swimming pool during my childhood lessons, drip onto my shorts. I wipe a cloth diaper over my eyes and the wet patch under my nose, then drop my forehead to the steering wheel. The song about gray days is over. He's gone, I think, I'll never see him again and I need him. I need a friend like that, a guy friend, honest and admiring. I have many women friends, handfuls actually, from different times in my life. There are the old friends, from high school and college, whom I depended on when we shared lives and homes, but with whom I share mostly small talk and reminiscences now. There are the local friends, with whom I compare notes on preschools and pediatricians, but who don't really know me. And there are the best friends, three women who know me to the core. Two, Lauren and Carrie, live far away and can only help me over the phone. The other one, Kelly, is a daily presence. But I am afraid to tell her how badly I'm feeling, except to describe the insomnia. I am afraid I will lose her if she knows that I'm really a mess inside and that I always have been.

Years ago, in tenth grade, three girls I'd opened my heart to dumped me. I still don't know why. One day we were a gang of best friends lying on the shag green carpet of one girl's bedroom. Within a week, they didn't want anything to do with me. Ever since, I've held a hand over my heart in dealings with all women. Later, when I'm at my lowest point, I will move that hand slightly as I lean hard on my women friends. They will see my softest spot and do nothing but protect it. Then, I will appreciate their value. But now I still don't trust them. Men, on the other hand, haven't betrayed me in friendship. I've always felt safer with them, which is probably why I miss Tom so much. The words, "I can't go on without him," don't come to mind. I don't think that silly, desperate thought. But I feel it.

O verreaction to passing emotions isn't my only symptom these days. There are also the evil twins that have plagued me all my life in times of stress: anxiety and diarrhea. One day, I push Max and Carrie in the double stroller down the street to a neighbor's house. It is overcast and breezy, as usual. Except for the day Wendy visited, the sun has been truant most of the season; instead it is a damp and rainy March of a summer. Still, I am sweating. I am pushing this chariot, which I've figured out weighs about seventy pounds carrying both of them, as fast as I can. I worry that the sharp, sudden pains in my lower abdomen will force me to have an accident in the middle of the neighborhood. I must be getting sick, I tell myself. I get this pain and rumbling when I have a stomach bug or I'm nervous. But there is nothing to make me nervous about this situation. I will drop Carrie off to play at her friend Kayla's, stay a few minutes to talk with her mother, Barrie, then push Max back home as I've done countless times before.

When we get to their house, I excuse myself to go to the bathroom. My digestive system empties. After I flush, a sickening smell hangs in the air, evidence of my loss of control. I close the bathroom door behind me, hoping Barrie won't go in there, humiliated at the thought that she will.

Another day, I stand abruptly in my friend Andrea's kitchen and announce that I must leave immediately. I cannot seem to wish or reason away the anxiety attack that besieged me moments earlier. Though I've had anxiety attacks many times before, there's always been a trigger: feeling trapped in a stuffy classroom or entering a building where I am about to submit to a job interview. The worst one of my life happened as I walked down the aisle to get married. I'd been calm all day—too calm, as if I'd taken a few of the muscle relaxants my mother offered me. I started to get nervous in the 1930s DeSoto as I rode to the synagogue with my maid of honor, Hilary. When we arrived, everyone but I had to go upstairs for a quick rehearsal. I couldn't join the rest of the wedding party because I didn't want Dave to see me before the ceremony. I was left in an office all alone, which is where the normal nervousness started to rev into overdrive. By the time Hilary and I tiptoed up an outside staircase and through a back kitchen, my stomach was starting to flip. Then my father took my arm and we headed down the aisle. Halfway down, I realized the wrong music was playing. Something had gone wrong. Something was out of place in the suitcase I had so carefully packed. I started to decompose inside. Anxiety crawled through my body like a dye shot into my spinal cord. I climbed three stairs with my husband-to-be and stood under a canopy of white lilies and tulle, shaking. I bent my knees one at a time so I wouldn't faint. My face turned green. Dave took stock of the guests behind us to make sure there was a doctor there who could revive me if I fainted. He gripped my wet hand and smiled nervously at me. Finally, after about five minutes, my heart slowed to a trot, the sweat glands shut their faucets, and my large intestine remembered its manners. I endured the rest of the ceremony in a state of aftershock, exhausted from the fight-or-flight reaction my body had had to marriage.

But now there is no reason for anxiety. The children are playing one room away. Andrea and I are talking about babies and drinking seltzer water from handblown green glasses just as we have whenever I've visited for the five years I've known her. But the classic symptoms layer on top of one another. Sweaty palms, shortness of breath, distraction, panic, my heart pumping blood faster than my veins can transport it, nausea. I make an excuse and gather up the kids. Thank God there are no winter coats to put on; thank God we are in the car moments after I announce our departure.

After my stomach and nerves have betrayed me enough times, I attempt to control these symptoms. I don't eat much besides bites of bland, white foods: rice, dry cereal, bananas, scrambled eggs, and Raman noodles. I don't spend time with other people in confined spaces. I stop going to friends' houses or inviting them to mine. I stop scheduling play dates for Carrie or inviting guests over for dinner. I alter my life so that I only go out in public places, where I am anonymous and can escape or fall apart at any time without anyone knowing. Deprivation and isolation, two more evil twins that conspire during depression, have joined my team.

But not all days are bad. Some, as is typical in most cases of PPD, are perfectly normal. (In all depressions, outside factors such as the amount of sleep you've gotten the night before or the degree of stress in the day affect how badly you feel.) Some days are so normal, in fact, that they disarm me. I think I've gotten past whatever's been my problem, and that all of the days to follow will be as smooth. So I make plans. Two days after Carrie starts camp, I plan to take Max clothes shopping. This was always one of my favorite activities with Carrie and I assume I will recapture the tranquillity of her baby days by doing it with Max. I will take him to a children's store with aisles and aisles of bright, soft clothes. He needs summer things, and Carrie needs new sneakers.

I love to shop. Malls have always calmed me, though while I am recovering from PPD, they will only stress me with sensory overload. I spent a lot of time in malls with my mother when I was young. She would take me shopping in expensive department stores and buy me whatever I wanted, even though she bought her own clothes in discount stores. I would kiss her cheek after the purchase was made, and we would walk to the escalator hand in hand, even when I was too old to be doing such things in public. It was a safe place for us, away from the chaos of our home, the volatility of my hot-tempered father. Years later, when I lived in a strange city with few friends, I would go to the mall by myself after work whenever I felt lonely. In that anonymous, generic space, I would feel safe.

So I am excited about this planned excursion with Max. But before we go, a woman who has hired me to edit a newsletter she publishes is coming over. We've planned an early meeting, so I'll have most of the morning for shopping. I've never edited before, but the money Dana will pay me will cover the cost of Max's child care. She's told me the work will only take twenty-four hours a month, so I see no reason to refuse. Today she will go over the newsletter and my job responsibilities with me.

After I drop Carrie off, I speed down the curving main road of our town to buy homemade, butter-laden blueberry muffins at the farm stand. I make it home in time to brew some coffee, put the dirty dishes in the sink, and settle Max into a flying saucer–like contraption. It sits on the floor, but rocks and swivels on its base when the baby moves. Max stands in the harness and plays with the toys on the tray that surrounds him. He can spend hours in this thing, hammering with rattles and soaking stuffed animals with saliva.

Once he's giggling away, I try to read the newspapers while I wait for Dana. It is Wednesday, food section day in the *Boston Globe* and the *New York Times*. I look at the pictures of plates stacked high with pyramids of multicolored food, then restlessly flip through the other sections. I used to read both papers cover to cover. Since Max's birth, I've rarely gotten through an entire article.

Dana is supposed to arrive by nine-thirty, but at five of ten, she calls to say it will be another half-hour. My morning is wasting away. When she finally arrives, she small talks over the muffins and coffee before spreading sample newsletters across the dining room table. We're acquaintances, having met through a Jewish women's organization several years earlier. Normally, I'd enjoy comparing notes on our two new babies, but today I'm impatient. She explains what she expects me to do with the newsletter, but I don't grasp much of it. I'm too tired to concentrate on something I'm not interested in to begin with (the newsletter is for a health-care union) and I'm worried. Worried that Max will start wailing soon. Worried that I won't have time to shop later. Worried that there's no way I'll be able to do this job, which she has just said will have to be completed each month over three consecutive days. I'd thought I could fit the work in at my leisure, but now it will be at her demand. The way my schedule is arranged, I will never have three days in a row to work without kids to take care of. And she wants me to start next month, before Carrie is in school and Wendy starts working.

I should just tell her I can't do the work. I should tell her I need to go out with Max so I have to cut the meeting short. But my thinking is muddled. I don't see obvious solutions, only new problems. Dana continues to talk, as if she's in the company of a normal person who can focus on conversation. Focus isn't one of my functioning skills these days. Just looking at a person's face for longer than a minute or two and trying to keep track of what they're saying wears me out. I get an overwhelming type of headache, the kind one gets after too many hours of studying or being in a museum, as if a layer of gauze is wrapped around the brain and it can't breathe. Dana obviously planned to spend the morning here. Even when I finally tell her my shopping plans, she makes no move to leave. I start sweating, then pacing between the table and the flying saucer. Can't she see I need to leave? Can't she see I need my life back?

When finally she packs her papers into a folder and goes, it is time for lunch. It is too late to do anything for myself.

All day and into the night I am furious at her for consuming my morning and for dumping the unexpected schedule on me. It's irrational, of course. Nothing is her fault; I should have been more assertive. Still, I feel trapped. Because I've committed to doing Dana's work, I really *need* child care for Max. I'm not sending him to day care and hiring Wendy simply so I can enjoy writing. Now I need them so I can do this job. And that is really why I'm upset. Dana's visit has cemented the child-care issue into place. Cement. Like quicksand or shoes around my feet.

Why don't you go to the bookstore," Dave says that night. "Just do something to relax."

He is worried about me, because I'm not sleeping and because I seem to be "a mess." He doesn't allow himself the luxury of specific worries; he just lives with an overwhelming feeling that something isn't right at home. He leaves for work later than usual and comes home earlier to help me with the kids. He believes, as I do, that that's all I need. He is buying all the excuses I come up with: I need more sleep or more coffee or more time to myself. A trip to the bookstore falls into that category.

He will tell me later that he was hoping my condition was just something I'd get through, that I was just having a hard time. It's a common state of denial for many husbands of PPD sufferers. First of all, most don't know anything about the illness. Second, who wants to face the fact that the mother of his baby is cracking up? It's easier to believe the best, that it's just a phase. There's a readily available excuse for everything. Sure I'm losing weight rapidly, but I'm running around a lot and don't have time to sit down for complete meals. Sure I'm seeing fewer people, but I'm so busy at home with those two kids! I enable Dave's denial by putting my best maternal face on. I tell him how badly I feel physically, but not how unsure I am that I can take care of the kids. I don't want him to think I can't handle it, to think I'm a failure. Parenting is my realm, the only area in our relationship where I feel I'm superior to him. It's a matter of pride to maintain that status. And there's also the issue of vulnerability. It's okay with me if Dave knows I'm neurotic—I'm pretty open with him about my worries and baggage—but if he thinks I'm a complete kook, who knows if he'll stick around. It's foolish of me, though, to think I can completely hide my problems from him. The changes in me are pretty hard to miss even if what they herald remains obscured.

When he suggests the bookstore, I am hunched in a family room chair, waiting for the fury of the day to dissipate. If the knob that controls my perspective rusted away earlier, now the dimmer switch that turns down emotions seems to be stuck. I have been possessed by this anger toward the editing job for hours. I can't let it go; can't move on to a less draining feeling.

I drive to the bookstore, buy a bestseller about a woman whose toddler is kidnapped, then head home, no more relaxed than before. A bath will do it, I decide, so I gather all my tools. The inflatable pillow that suctions to the back of the tub, fleecy pink robe, purple towel, new book, and soft orange spheres filled with scented herbs reputed to calm. I drop two of the orange balls into the bath water. The faucet drums hot water on top of them, rupturing their skins and releasing beads of oil and promises of relaxation. I enter next, the steaming water hot enough to scald my feet, the way I like it. I crouch in the water until I'm brave enough to lower my behind to the floor of the tub, stretch out my legs, and lie back on the pillow. My breasts stay dry, perched on top of my chest. They are as full and round as they would be if they contained silicone instead of milk. But they are the only fleshy part of me. The slack skin on my belly, so recently stretched to its limits, caves toward my pelvis. My ribs and sternum, collarbones and hips are visible. Though I have always been short and thin, ninety-seven pounds looks good on no one. I don't remember skipping meals, nor do I remember eating them. I must just pick at whatever I put on my plate and have lost weight without noticing.

I relax enough in the bath to go to bed and fall asleep quickly. Then the soldier prods me awake with the butt of his gun. There is a soldier on watch living inside of me, one who won't stand for deep sleep lest I miss something. Max is what I could miss. What if he needs me and I don't hear him because I'm asleep? I feel this soldier pulling me out of sleep as surely as if he were pulling me by the collar out of a foxhole whenever I start to drift. *Don't do it,* I hear him say, *don't give into it.* This imaginary man has been my nighttime partner since the insomnia started. He is young and wiry, with a turned-up nose and sharp chin. Big eyes peer from under his giant bowl of a helmet. He has walked out of a 1944 issue of *Life* magazine to make sure I follow orders. It's my job to stay awake, to be on the alert for any sign that my son needs me. *You snooze, you lose,* the soldier orders. I lose my son. If I sleep, I lose my son.

I run my hand up Dave's thigh to wake him. It works. He's used to me waking him so he can help me get back to sleep. But tonight I want more. I lie on top of him and run my hands over his graying chest hair. I want to make love, like a normal woman. And we do. And I do feel normal, for the few minutes we are connected. I forget about the insomnia, the emotions, the drain, the homesickness, the shaking from within. At the end, only one of us sinks back to sleep.

I have vowed not to take anything to help me sleep that could seep from my bloodstream into Max's breast milk. I have been tempted, on so many nights, to buy sleeping pills. Oh, they would solve the whole problem, I think. But I can't expose my baby to barbiturates. But maybe something natural, I decide tonight, maybe that won't be so bad.

Dave has some melatonin tablets in a kitchen cabinet that he'd bought in preparation for a business trip to Japan. The natural hormone is marketed to help travelers reset their internal clocks and bring on sleep when they cross time zones. Though having a newborn is like traveling to a place where morning and night arrive at unfamiliar times, my body has not adjusted. I seem constantly tuned to wake-up mode. Maybe this will balance me.

I wake Dave again to ask what he thinks.

"How many hours until you nurse again?"

"Like five or six," I say.

"Try a half," he says, his voice raspy with sleep. "It should be out of your system by then."

So I take the pill. And while I'm down in the kitchen, I pour myself a bowl of Cheerios and milk. When I was pregnant and woke up starving, I ate a bowl in the middle of most nights. The rings of wheat and sugar filled my stomach and the tryptophan-laden milk wooed me to sleep as soon as I rested my cheek on the pillow. Tonight, there is no such luck. Neither the pill nor the food helps. Sleep doesn't come until near sunrise. Four hours, that night, is all my body gets.

The kids and I are supposed to meet my friend Kelly and her two sons at the lake the next morning. The plan is to meet midmorning, feed the kids a picnic lunch, and leave at naptime. I call her to alter the schedule.

"We're only gonna stay for an hour," I say. "I can't deal with the whole lunch thing."

"How about this," she says. "I'll pack lunch for your kids. Then you won't have to worry about it."

Kelly is a psychotherapist. She knows how to help people and has no hang-ups doing so.

"You'd do that for me?" I say, trying to sound coy but really incredulous that anyone would do something so helpful.

"Of course," she says, laughing a little. "It's no problem. I just want you to meet us there."

By the time we arrive, Kelly and her kids are camped by the water's edge. Carrie runs down to join them and I settle Max in his car seat into a patch of shade under a tree. He's sleeping, so I take a low beach chair down to the water and sit next to Kelly.

She's talking with another woman and stops to introduce me. I'd hoped we could be alone. I don't feel very well, so I don't even try to thread my thoughts into their conversation. My head is heavy and my fingertips are tingling. The rims of my eyes feel raw. My heart seems to be beating in slow motion, as if it has to think about it extra hard before making the effort.

I glance back at Max. He's drenched in sun! The earth is moving so quickly that he's losing his shade. I go up to move him, return to the water, then bring my chair back up to the tree. I feel better being closer to him, to battle the sun and anyone who might want to kidnap him. I look down the slope of the beach and see all the other people living their lives: women talking, children playing. And I see myself, all alone under a tree, as disconnected from everyone else as I've ever felt. *Please come up here to sit with me,* I think to Kelly. *Please come up here to dry off,* I think to the kids. *I don't want to be alone.*

If I were one of those people who could ask for help, who could tell people when she's afraid to be on a patch of sand alone, I would weather my bout of PPD better. But I'm not one of those people. I'm the type who waits for others to offer help. It's hard to wait much longer, though.

"Do I seem normal to you?" I ask Kelly when she finally joins me. Maybe she will tell me I don't. Maybe she will use her powers of friendship and professional experience to make me well again.

The kids are sitting on one towel eating peanut butter and jelly sandwiches. Carrie wears the Big Sister T-shirt over her bathing suit. Max nurses.

"Yeah," she says. "You seem really tired and kind of stressed, but that's understandable. You still seem normal."

Good, I think. I feel terrible, but I guess I'm still okay or Kelly would know it. But how could she? I am ashamed of myself, but I can't bear for the people who love me to be ashamed of me. So I hide my weakness with the desperation of a shoplifter hiding a stolen lipstick. I've always been what they call a "high-functioning" depressive. After a lifetime of pushing myself to appear perfect, I'm an expert. I accomplish everything I need to without anyone knowing I'm terrified inside. People see what I achieve, not what I avoid out of irrational fear. I've known how to ice skate since I was three years old and once showed enough promise that my parents hired a private instructor for me. But I've never had the guts to attempt the simplest spin. In fourth grade, I was so afraid to go to school that my mother had to tell the teacher to watch out for me; knowing she was keeping her eye on me gave me the security to get through the day. But the kids never knew. I still stole hats at recess and scolded the fat kid next to me for breathing too loud. In college, when I was seeing a therapist and eating only plain noodles for every meal, I managed to make it to classes and parties so no one suspected I was in rough shape. If anyone had seen me going to the mental health office of the health clinic, I planned to tell them I was there to do a story for journalism class. Even at my wedding, only Dave and his brother realized how anxious I was. And when I tell friends later that I had PPD this summer, most are shocked. "You seemed fine," they say, because my charade is a success.

I will come to believe that PPD is not something that is obvious to anyone but experts in the field. It is not a disease that announces itself boldly. Rather, its symptoms weave themselves into the fabric of the normal stresses of early motherhood. All new mothers are tired, pale, and easily stressed. How can one tease apart those characteristics from the ails of PPD unless they've been through it or specialize in it? On the outside, the signs of PPD are so subtle that loved ones would have to be looking for them to discover something other than garden variety new-motherhooditis. So even though Kelly is an expert in counseling the worried well, she has not treated any PPD. And even though Dave loves and knows me, he knows nothing of the beast that faces him daily. This is how I manage to keep my foundering mental state a secret for so long.

That night, I give up on the bed. For weeks, I haven't been able to sleep there, despite squeezing Dave's hand, clutching my childhood security blanket, and forcing myself to play exhausting mind games. I've tried thinking of a different person's name beginning with each letter of the alphabet until I reach Zelda or Zeke and kick the mattress in frustration. I've counted backward from 100. I've even attempted math problems, once a sure way to bring on sleep. I've snapped on my Itty Bitty Nite Lite, picked up the novel that lay open on the floor next to me, and read about the kidnapped boy until I felt tired. Then I've closed the book, snapped off the light, lowered my eyelids and laid there.

So, tonight I am trying it on the couch. I've dragged my pillow and blankets down to the family room and set up a nest. I sink into the couch, its overstuffed cushions covered with navy blue cotton as soft and smooth as worn khakis, and I click on the television. A late-night talk program, with a host I've read about many times but never seen because his show starts so deep into the night, interviews an actress who leans her breasts over his desk and cackles as if she's drunk. Then the eleven o'clock news runs again. I've already seen it once. Then Andy Griffith pretending to be a country lawyer. I clamp my eyes shut and roll from side to front to stomach. A buzzing sensation that has been pulsing through my body all night won't cease. It feels as if I'm on uppers, black beauties, or No-Doz, but the opposite is true. I moderated my position on alcohol and breast milk and drank a beer before bed. Then I ate cereal soaked in milk an hour into my insomnia. I tried another half of a melatonin after that. When nothing has changed an hour later, I take a small brown glass jar from the medicine shelf in the kitchen. Valerian, an herb known to work the same way Valium does, without any side effects or addiction, has to solve this problem. I squeeze a dropperful of the bitter liquid into tap water and swallow it. I lie back on my blankets and sing over and over the lullaby my mother sang to me when I'd had a bad dream. *Go to sleepy little baby. Go to sleepy little baaaby. When you wake, we'll patty patty cake. And ride a shiny little pony.*

The song and the herb don't sedate me, so I reach behind the milk cartons in the refrigerator and pull out an old bottle of chardonnay. I pour the pale gold acid into a juice glass, carry it to my nest and chug it.

But the buzz only gets louder. Nothing, it seems, will stop it. I can't stand to be alone anymore, stranded in the middle of this night. There are too many hours before dawn, too many minutes of this feeling to endure. I haven't slept for more than a few hours for the past two nights. This is the third. What if I don't sleep at all tonight? What will happen to me then? What happens to a body when it doesn't work right for so long? I'm too scared to think of the answer. I wish there were somewhere I could go, to find someone to help me. I feel too guilty to wake Dave yet again. If there were a twenty-four-hour pharmacy nearby, I'd drive to it. If there were a neighbor's light on, I'd knock on the door. I wish the people from the TV could smash through the glass and come sit on the couch with me.

I climb the stairs and stand by Dave.

"You have to come down with me," I whisper. "I can't sleep and I'm scared and I need you to help me."

Dave rises without complaint and follows me to the couch. Whenever he gets up with me he is a soothing presence that eventually coaxes me back to bed. He usually strokes my hair and tells me that everything will be okay in a voice so filled with confidence and tenderness that I believe him. Tonight though, we sit on opposite corners of the couch, cross-legged and straight-backed. I ramble.

"I think I want to call your mother," I say. "She always has insomnia. She'll know what to do. She'll understand."

"You can't call my mother." He looks annoyed.

"Why not? She won't mind. She'll understand."

"It's too late. It's after three in the morning. You just can't do that, Sue."

He is usually nicer than this. I just want reassurance that what I'm going through is normal. If he won't let me get it from his mother, he'll have to give it to me. We sit in quiet for a minute. I move closer to him, sit on my knees like a child.

"Do you think I'm having a nervous breakdown?"

I know he will say no. I know he will balance my hysteria with his reason, as he always does, and calm me down and hold me until I sleep. I know it. He will tell me I'm okay, and I will stop worrying.

"I don't know," he says, staring at me, his eyes suddenly ignited with a fear I've never seen there.

I don't know? You ask your husband if you're on your way to the loony bin and he says *I don't know?*

If there is one thing clear now it is this: nothing and nobody is going to make everything all right.

I cry when I hear his statement, cry hard because he answers in an affirmative the question I've been asking myself all summer. I am having a nervous breakdown. All these problems—with sleeping and focusing and maintaining a grip on myself—have been symptoms of my mind's unraveling. Now there is no denying, no rationalizing, no escaping. It's finally happened, the thing I've held off all my life. I'm in the midst of a breakdown, with a terrified husband and two completely dependent children. I have no idea what comes next.

When I finally fall asleep curled in the corner of the couch, there are three hours before morning. And when business starts for the rest of the world, I am on the phone to my doctor.

Chapter 4

The air is gray, hot and heavy, as if it can be parted and stepped through to a better place. It is the morning after my first official meeting with mental illness and I am walking to kill time before my doctor appointment. I walk past chemically nourished green lawns in front of homes abandoned for the day. We live in the Bird Streets, a development of charmless Colonials and boxy split level ranches built in the seventies about two miles from the tiny center of town. The eagles, owls, hawks, and ravens the streets were named for disappeared after the woods that had been their home were scraped away to make room for the roads and streetlights and underground electric wiring. It usually appears that the human inhabitants have migrated as well. No passing cars force me onto the sidewalks, and though it is summer vacation, there are no children licking Popsicles on front steps or riding bikes up and down the driveways. They go to camp now, all day, every day, so each street is as vacant as an alley.

This is one of the countless walks I take during these July days. Through the neighborhood in the morning and at dusk, to the lake on weekends, accompanied by the stroller or the dog or just the stories I weave in my mind of women who walk away from their families forever. Today I imagine a woman who lives near an airport extending a neighborhood walk into an escape. She marches straight out of her development, past the cabs delivering vacationers to the airport, and into a terminal, charging a ticket on the credit card she happens to have in her pocket. To Hawaii. Or Tahiti. Or London, to hide in a pub with a stack of books. Just a story, I tell myself, but I'm still grateful that there isn't an airport within walking distance of my house.

A real woman on Cape Cod has walked away from her life this summer. The mother of three with a history of depression was on vacation with her family. One evening, she bathed her two-year-old and told her mother-in-law she was going to a gas station to vacuum the sand out of the car. The next morning, they found the car near a deserted patch of shore, but to this day have not seen her again. She left a note saying she thought she was a bad mother and that her family would be better off without her. Her tall, sad-eyed husband appeals for her return every night on the news and so do I. She terrifies me, this escapee, because I know exactly how she felt as she drove away. It is how I feel now, like a failure who just wants to leave all this responsibility behind. And I am so scared that I will lose complete control of my sensible mind and do what she did, leaving my beautiful kids and sweet husband forever. Proving once and for all what a disappointment I am to them.

It isn't until much later in the year that I realize I am trying to outdistance my pain with all these walks. I'd done the same thing the morning after I'd broken up with my first love twelve years earlier. I walked vigorously that day, off campus, through woods and public gardens of blue perennials until I was exhausted. But the ache in my chest hadn't subsided until months later. I couldn't simply walk it off. And now, on the day I am supposed to be acknowledging my nervous breakdown, I am still trying to play tag with my pain. If I keep moving, maybe it will lose track of me and quit the pursuit altogether.

My doctor appointment isn't until later this morning. I called my primary care physician at nine and described my symptoms to the receptionist: can't sleep, always anxious, might be some sort of postpartum thing. I don't know why I suspect postpartum depression before I know anything about it. My only guess is that those words had been embedded in my brain years before, when I was pregnant with Carrie. I was reading a copy of the *Boston Parents Paper,* studying each advertisement for preschools, new mothers' groups, and family vacation resorts when an ad for Depression After Delivery (DAD) stopped me like a roadblock. That's horrible, I remember thinking. Imagine being depressed when you have a new baby. Imagine the feelings of failure you'd have if you were depressed when you were supposed to be so happy. Then in a quieter voice, deep down: *imagine if that's when it gets me.*

Maybe I knew I was a PPD case waiting to happen; maybe that's why the ad scared me so. To guard against having to call the Depression After Delivery number, I took proactive steps before I delivered Carrie. I signed on with an organization that sends experienced mothers to spend an hour a week with new mothers. The Visiting Mom would know if I got depressed, I reasoned, so it couldn't creep up on me. Thankfully, I didn't need her surveillance, since I only experienced a two-week period of postpartum blues after Carrie's birth. But seeing that DAD ad and admitting, however subconsciously, that I could be vulnerable to such a depression have turned out to be stored nuggets of gold that are leading me to help now.

Dave has stayed home from work today, hoping that I will be able to get some medical help before the weekend starts. He wants me, at this point, to just solve the problem. He thought all this trouble was something I would get over, not something that would spiral out of control. And he is finally realizing that patting me on the head and promising me I'll be fine might not be enough. He might actually have to start picking up pieces soon.

"I'm scared," I tell him after I return from my walk.

"I'm scared, too," he says.

"Why? Don't you think I'm going to be okay?" I believe Dave speaks in fact, that everything he says is the truth. He is extremely intelligent and always seems to know the right answer when it involves heating systems or mutual funds. I assume whatever he opines about me will be equally irrefutable. However he answers this question will be my truth.

"Well, I think so, but I don't want it to get out of hand so I'm stuck raising two kids."

"What do you think is going happen to me?"

A good friend of ours attempted suicide a few months earlier. I know it is on both of our minds.

"Not that," he says.

Then what? I wonder. *Does he think I'll be committed?*

"You're the glue that holds us together," he says, putting his panic away. "We need you. I just want you to feel better."

My primary care doctor leads me past the examining rooms and into his office, offers me a seat in a freshly upholstered chair and asks what's going on. He's a young guy, tall and thin with tightly curled blond hair, whom I've been seeing for a few years for routine physicals and sore throats.

"You need a vacation," he says after I finish telling him about the past four months, "two days alone, without any responsibilities except to sleep and eat. You need to take care of yourself."

"Well, I'm still nursing, so I can't really go away now."

"And I'd suggest some counseling. You need a long-term plan for managing your stress. It's very hard taking care of kids. What you need is a system."

He laces his fingers together and holds his linked hands up, a visual to demonstrate the harmony I'll have once I devise this system. I smile and nod and agree with his suggestions. He is giving me answers, which is exactly what I had sought. That they are the wrong ones doesn't matter to me now.

Finally, he prescribes the magic bullet: Benadryl.

"It'll help you sleep," he says. "Call me if you need something stronger. If not, come back in a month and we'll see how you're doing then."

Benadryl! All I've needed all this time is Benadryl? Why hadn't I thought of that? Of course antihistamines will put me to sleep. I'm not having a nervous breakdown after all. I just need a cold medicine.

I practically skip across the street to the pharmacy to buy my magic potion, then dance through the door to our house to give Dave the good news. In true PPD fashion, I am in the throes of a mood swing. Just as PPD brings with it good and bad days, there are also good and bad hours. Now I luxuriate in the unfamiliar feeling of control. I am absolutely sure I am about to recover completely. *This was just a temporary thing that you worried much too much about, as usual,* I tell myself. *It'll turn out to be nothing.* I am so relieved that the doctor did not declare me crazy that I actually take an afternoon nap. A whole hour of deep, relaxing sleep, proving again how well I am already.

Alas, the Benadryl capsule that floats down my throat on a wave of tap water does nothing but harm. Drugs often have the opposite affect on me. In my recreational drug use days, cocaine would make me withdraw until I felt I was watching the world from behind a screen door. Alcohol would energize me, without ever dropping me later. In keeping with this trend, the antihistamine makes me more hyper than usual instead of sleepy. The label says it can cause hyperactivity in children. And me.

The next morning I rise to see darkness out of every window. Had a playwright crafted my story, the weather settings would have been too corny to believe. But on this day after another turbulent night, there are hurricane warnings throughout the region. Heavy rain keeps us indoors, where the kids watch TV and I sit in the corner of the couch. I am afraid to move, scared that too much motion will pop the bubbles of anxiety resting in every cavity of my body, sending a mist of panic through every organ.

I manage to make it upstairs to my bed, where I call my friend Liz. She has told me that after she had her daughter she didn't think she could make it through the days, which were all dark. She realized later that she'd had PPD. I tell her about my murky days and about feeling I won't make it to the end of some of them. I tell her I can't sleep and that I'm always nervous. Does this sound the same? Yes, she says.

"It sucks," she says. "It really sucks."

"So, how did you get better?" I ask.

"I went to California."

She paints a pretty picture: emerging from the grim cold days of New England to the bright, warm ones of the West coast, she took walks with her baby outside every day. She ate well and slept late. The change in time zones and weather patterns was the beginning of her recovery. It feels good to hear her story. I feel safe, as if my blond friend with the dangly earrings is sitting on my bed with me. I want to keep her on the phone all day.

"How did you make it when you felt this bad?" I ask. "What did you do all day?"

"I just watched the clock and waited for Rick to come home," she says.

"Do you think I'm gonna be okay?"

She tells me I will, eventually, feel normal again. Every word she says soothes me because she understands. I don't want her to leave me, but she has a life to return to. In a few minutes, she has to take her daughter to a birthday party. We say good-bye. I hold the phone to my ear until I hear the line click to nothing. Alone again, I lie back on my bed and cry. When will this end?

After dropping Carrie at camp on Monday, I try once again to get myself some help. On Friday, the doctor had told me to pick up some therapists' business cards from his receptionist on my way out. Today I leave messages with every one of them. Even though the doctor failed me with his Benadryl cure, that doesn't mean they will. I call the breast pump rental lady and ask if she knows any therapists who specialize in postpartum depression. She digs through some papers and gives me the name two DAD contacts. I call the first, a woman named Karen who survived PPD in the eighties, when the only treatments available were Valium and time. Karen listens to my tale and gives me news I don't want to hear.

"Sounds like you need a psychiatrist," she says. "You need to be on medication."

So I am crazy after all.

She reads off a list of names and numbers of shrinks and nurse psychotherapists. I call them all, leaving brief but panicky messages with their receptionists or on their answering machines.

Late that afternoon I am in my kitchen with my mother when the phone rings. It is Kate Heineman, a nurse psychotherapist who specializes in postpartum issues. I tell her my problem.

"Can you come in tomorrow?" she asks.

My, I think, she's taking this awfully seriously. I must sound really bad. I take a two-thirty appointment. Only twenty-two hours to wait.

My mother is standing over a silver pan at the stove as I hang up the phone. She heats up sweet and sour meatballs my mother-in-law has sent over. Pepper is too weak to drive from Rhode Island to help me herself. If she weren't sick, she would be here daily, I know it, bringing Corning Ware crocks of food and soothing Max's cries. She is a giver, that Pepper, one of those people who knows exactly how to help. I love her for that, but these days I'm angry and frustrated that she can't help me. I need her to take care of us, but the cancer in her bowels is keeping her from us. Still, she manages to ease my stress in her absence. Her donations of tiny meatballs soaked in a marriage of tomato and cranberry sauce save me from having to cook.

My mother, Doris, comes once or twice a week from her

home in Rhode Island to try to help me take care of the kids. Sometimes she brings dinner. Sometimes she plays with Max while I try to nap, but I always end up stomping into the nursery and yelling at her for not knowing how to keep him from crying. Once she even sleeps on the pull-out couch because I am tired of waking Dave in the middle of the night, but still so afraid of being alone with my insomnia. Knowing she is a flight of stairs away, knowing that if I need to I can crawl into bed with her just as Carrie nuzzles with me after a bad dream, allows me to have a peaceful night's sleep. The night after she stays at my house, she calls me before bed.

"Can I call you if I need to talk?" I ask, before hanging up.

"Anytime."

"Even in the middle of the night if I can't sleep?"

"I'll be right by the phone. Call whenever you need, Sweetie."

Tonight, as I sit down to eat, Mom gets ready to leave. And as she walks out the door and leaves me alone with my children, I want to run to her, hang on her skirt, cry "Mommy" into her bosom. PPD mothers need to be mothered more than any other women, though I don't know this yet. I only know it is strange for me to yearn for my mother. For years I've turned my face from her kisses and cut short her phone calls. Though I considered her my best friend for most of my childhood, I have spent my adulthood pulling away from her in an attempt to guard my independence. Our relationship has been a pendulum of unhealthy attachment: too close for a mother and child, too distant for a mother and woman. But now all I want is for her to lift me into her lap and rock me in the black wooden rocking chair that sat in my childhood bedroom. I need to be taken care of, but don't yet know how to ask.

Kate Heineman gets paid to take care of me, for fifty minutes at least. The next afternoon I drive to a quaint upscale neighborhood where her office occupies a room three floors up in an old building. I have brought Max with me because there is no one to watch him today. I lug his car seat up two flights of a dark, stuffy staircase, pulling myself along on the elegant wooden banister until I reach the top, where a skylight shines dust motes on a metal patio chair. Inside Kate's office, an airy space with lavender walls, I sit in a black leather swivel chair across from an identical one that she occupies. Max sits in his car seat by my side, fingering toys, drinking a bottle of breast milk, flirting with Kate. Her shiny black Portuguese water dog, Rosie, sits in the corner. When Rosie stirs, Kate squirts water at him from a plastic lemon without ever moving her eyes from my face.

She has short whitish-gray hair, an impish smile, and the wind-kissed skin of someone who spends entire summers on sailboats. She asks, as most therapist do at the start of session number one, what has brought me here today. With those words spoken in that soft, kind voice, all the sandbags that had been keeping the flood of my pain at bay slide away. Everything I've been feeling, everything I've let out only in leaks to Dave or Kelly or Mom gushes from me in a surge of words and tears interrupted only when I need to blow my nose. I tell her about Wendy and Dana and work and day care and Pepper's cancer and feeling so tired and obsessing and the miscarriages. I list all the other ingredients of my meltdown: my lack of steady help with the kids; my disappointment that the difficulties of the last two years didn't melt into euphoria as soon as Max hit three months, my personal and family history of depression.

I tell her that my parents have both taken antidepressants and that I've been in and out of short-term therapy most of my life. I've grown from a kid with constant stomachaches and a fear of leaving her mother's side to an adult with frequent anxiety attacks and a need for perfection that has stunted my personal and professional growth. I haven't yet learned that depression is hereditary, so I blame my parents' problems on a lack of coping skills and tell myself I'm nothing like them.

I tell her about my history with shrinks: I've gone to one every few years of my life since I was eight. It will become clear to me later that I'd always suffered from low-level depression (officially called dysthymia). Had antidepressants, SSRIs in particular, been around in the sixties, I probably would have had a much richer and more satisfying childhood. But exploring the psychological reasons for emotional difficulties has been in vogue for most of my life. So each time I had terrible stomachaches or anxiety, I was taken or took myself to a licensed social worker or psychologist who always found a juicy problem to solve. The counselor I saw when I was eight baked banana bread with me and told me I was afraid to grow up. At sixteen, I was told I was simply a pawn between my feuding parents. During junior year of college my favorite therapist—a young man who dared to wear both a tie and an earring in one lobe and who didn't take any crap from me—informed me that I hadn't learned to be human. In my midtwenties, I needed help extracting myself from a stale relationship. After Carrie was born the counselor I saw to work out my "stress" decided all the dynamics of my family of origin needed dissecting.

I emerged from each short-term session cured of whatever problem I'd brought to the table. The therapist would tell me what was wrong and then he or she would tell me how to fix it. But because my brain was probably never up to the task, I didn't gain the skills necessary to identify and solve my own problems. And none of the therapists ever got to the heart of the matter: life was so hard for me because I was clinically depressed. I never considered my problems anything other than blemishes I could—and should—erase. Not knowing anything about brain chemistry and the biochemical reasons for depression, I always viewed my constant state of angst as a character flaw. If I'm this unhappy, I must be doing something wrong, I told myself most of my life. Even as a child, I berated myself for being so sad and nervous. Usually, I kept my depressive symptoms concealed. But like a beach ball held under water, they were always threatening to bob to the surface. I lived with the unarticulated fear that one day a major connection would be severed and I would have a nervous breakdown.

I wonder, sometimes, what would have happened if one of them had uttered the words "clinical depression" or suggested a psychiatrist. Would I have gone into denial and continued to blame my behavior on specific life issues, or would I have felt relieved to have a name for my problems? Only one health-care professional got close to diagnosing me correctly, but even he failed to be specific enough. During college, when my stomach was again bothering me, my gastroenterologist told me if I didn't get psychological help, "I'd never make it." I was so angry with him that I cried for an entire weekend and never went back to him. I'd already gotten psychological help. Who was he to destine me to failure? *I'd show him,* I decided. *I'd be fine.* I guess you could call that denial.

I cry. It is the longest, hardest cry I've had in my entire adult life and it feels so good. I know I would be fine if I could stay in her office, safe and able to cry. But fifty minutes starts to close in on us. She tells me it sounds as if I have postpartum depression and that she strongly recommends antidepressants. But she won't give them to me until I'm ready to take them, she says, physically and emotionally.

First, I have to wean Max so he won't drink the brain-altering chemicals that seep into my breast milk. It is around this time, 1996, that researchers are discovering that it's safe to nurse while taking antidepressants, that babies exposed to the drugs have no adverse affects or developmental delays. But that information hasn't filtered down from the research journals to the practitioners like Kate yet, so she must tell me the standard party line: antidepressants and breast milk haven't been proven a harmless cocktail yet, so she won't prescribe Zoloft until I wean. By 1998, though researchers can't say that they are 100 percent certain that antidepressants have no affect on babies (more studies on infant brain chemistry are needed), they are confident enough to permit most women to nurse their brains with antidepressants and their babies with breast milk. It is safer, one prominent psychiatrist says, than the effect of maternal depression on the baby.

Though I don't want to wean (nursing is the only thing going well these days) the bigger hurdle is agreeing to take an antidepressant. The decision is up to me, Kate stresses. She won't force me to take it, and we can talk more about it at the next session.

Despite the evidence that I carry in my skull the type of brain for which antidepressants were created, I am completely against the idea. I know nothing about brain chemistry, how hormones regulate those chemicals, how those chemicals regulate mood, and how we humans have absolutely no control over our moods. I am blind to the science of it all, and am self-righteous as hell. In my mind, crazy people take antidepressants. Or people who don't have the skills to solve their problems the old-fashioned way. Weak people. People who don't try hard enough. My parents. I am not like them. I do not need a crutch, no matter how badly I feel. I've just been through a bad time, I tell myself.

Kate sends me on my way with a prescription for Klonopin, a sedating sleep aid, an appointment for later in the week, and a sheet of white copy paper printed with the words Depression Checklist on top. Below the title are twelve symptoms of depression. I will only glance at the list today, but later I will fill it out as if it were a survey, placing mental check marks by the symptoms that apply.

1. Sadness. Tearfulness. *Check.*
2. Discouragement. Hopelessness. *Check.*
3. Lack of concentration. Indecisiveness. *Check.*
4. Irritability. Resentment. Attacks of rage. *Check.*
5. Sleep increase or decrease. Weight loss or gain. *Decrease and loss.*
6. Appetite increase or decrease. *Decrease.*
7. Low energy. Lack of motivation. *Check.*

8. Suicidal thoughts. *Check*. Suicidal impulses or plan. *No*.
9. Anxiety. Panic attacks. Worry. Overwhelmed. Restlessness. *Check*.
10. Loss of interest in life. *No*.
11. Low self-esteem. Guilt. Failure. Feel worthless. Self-disparagement. *Check, check, check, check, check*.
12. Feel worse in morning or evening? *The same*.

I'm not crazy, I tell myself. I can't be crazy. Anyone would feel a little out of sorts if she'd had two years of stress and four months of sleep deprivation. If I'm crazy, I think ignorantly, if I have a mental illness, I will have to live in a mental hospital and never see my children again. I will officially be a failure. No, I'm not crazy. I just need to work harder. Depression may have dug its claws into me, but I *will* shake it off.

And that's what I set out to do. Over the next five weeks, I employ the following strategies to cure myself:

Wendy comes to babysit for us once. She plays lovingly with the kids, convincing Carrie to pick up the stuffed animals sprawled over her floor by creating a make-believe animal kingdom with her. I leave them to go to the supermarket and practically break into a musical-worthy soft-shoe by the deli counter because I feel so free. I'm alone! I can think! I can order American cheese without having to stick a pacifier into a gaping mouth! As I turn the corner to our street on the way home I am thinking about asking Wendy to add more hours to her schedule so I can have more freedom. Then I see Wendy walking with the kids, Carrie chatting by her side and Max in the stroller. My mood changes like an image rotated through a slide projector. Elated. *Click*. Furious. *Click*. Distraught. *How dare she take my kids for a walk without asking,* my crazy mind thinks. *She's got nerve to think she can take my place like that, making my kids happy while I'm away.* For the rest of the afternoon I count the hours until she leaves. When she does, a new layer of tension has draped over my shoulders like a lead apron.

I try to talk myself out of my resistance to using Wendy. On Saturday, I creep down to my mildewy basement office and type single-spaced pages of argument on the computer. Writing has always helped. Writing has always lead to a solution. But this time it only goes in circles: why I feel so bad about letting someone else watch my kids, why I shouldn't feel so bad, why I need outside child care, why I can't bear to let go of my full-time mom label, around and around and around. I stop writing when it is time to leave for a baby shower.

At a house in the woods with flowers stenciled on the walls and handmade quilts on the beds, my college roommate Kathy is celebrating the upcoming arrival of her first son. I immediately head for the liquor table on the deck. I haven't had more than two drinks at a time since I got married, but for many years before that alcohol served as a crust to contain my emotions. My hands are shaking and the ruminations about Wendy won't stop. My night-time obsessions have broken into daylight. A beer will help, I reason, reaching for the crutch so common to male depressives. But it takes such energy to bring the bottle to my lips that I don't get much of the bitter summer brew into my body. At one point in the afternoon, I leave the group and sit in a family room alone, looking at the sewing machine, thinking how superior the woman of this house is to me because she can make curtains and quilts. By the time we stuff the kids back into their car seats and leave, the buzz of anxiety is so intense I can barely sit. It is like physical pain that one tries to squirm away from. But I can't escape it. I have been trying for three days to find a road that will lead me to a comfortable place with the Wendy situation. But I have only exhausted and terrified myself, like someone stuck in a labyrinth. It is time to get out. I can't bear hitting dead ends any longer. As soon as we get home, I call Wendy and fire her. The schedule won't work, I tell her. Then relief floods over me like a hot shower, rinsing away the stress as if it were grime. It's over. I feel much better. I have myself back again.

The feeling lasts for one night.

Without Wendy to help me, there is no way I can do the editing job for Dana. I call her and quit. Relief returns. Lasts half a day.

I have called Marge Drake several times over the summer to talk about Max's day care. This time when I call, I tell her I want to bring him by a few times before he is scheduled to start so I can see if he is comfortable there. We haven't been to her house since he was a newborn. Seeing the place again, I'm sure, will make the transition easier for both of us.

She can't let me visit, she says, because she's closed for vacation in August. But she's on to me, before I'm even straight with myself.

"Are you thinking of not sending Max?" Marge asks over the phone.

"No, no, no, no," I reply, probably too quickly. "I'm just a little nervous about it. Are most mothers nervous before they send their first child to day care?"

"Yes," she says, "but not as anxious as you seem."

Two days later as I push Max in his stroller in front of the library, it hits me like a revelation that I don't have to send him to day care, that it's okay not to be ready. It also means, to my black-and-white thinking, that I'll never go back to work, will never achieve anything as a writer, will always be a loser. But I don't have the strength to fight with myself about that now. I just have to get this one last burr out of my paw. I call Marge to relinquish the slot. She is characteristically gracious, only thanking me for giving her enough notice to fill it with someone else. When Dave comes home that night, I greet him with a hug and a proud announcement.

"I'm better now," I say, completely serious. "I just wasn't ready to send Max to day care."

And I really believe the worst is over, that with one phone

call I have licked all my troubles. About two days later, when the anxiety and insomnia return, I move down the list of solutions.

Maybe walking isn't enough. Maybe I need some real exercise. One of the perks of my last newspaper job was a free membership to the YMCA in Somerville, New Jersey. It was there, after years of associating swimming with those terrifying lessons of my childhood, that I learned to love pulling my body through the womb of chlorine and tile. I started swimming with my head above the water, but one day a teenaged lifeguard taught me how to rotary breathe.

"Roll your body," the boy with tight muscles and hairless chest instructed from the side of the pool. "Rest your ear on the water. Don't pull your head up!"

I did laps every other day after work. The pool was never crowded and never cold. I had my little lifeguard savior to watch over me. I believe I was more relaxed that year than during any other of my life. There were other factors, of course. I had a prestigious, well-paying job, lots of friends, no steady boyfriend, and no family pressures, since I lived 300 miles away from any relatives. But the regular exercise—the scheduled endorphin high—had a lot to do with my happiness.

So, I decide to try it again. One morning I drive with Max to the Jewish Community Center one town over. If we join now, the lady in membership tells us, we get the rest of the summer for free. Plus, there's baby-sitting downstairs. I fill out the forms. I write a check. I visit the baby-sitting room.

Two women, one chubby and matronly and one with an earring in her nose, watch the children while their mothers exercise. "Yes," the matronly one says, "we have room for one more. Come back Monday at ten."

On Monday, I leave Max in her arms because she seems

competent and because I am so glad to give him away. I have an hour, a whole hour to myself! I head to the locker rooms and pull on my old blue Speedo. The first day, I manage ten lengths of the pool. As the weeks progress, I get to twenty. Max smiles continuously in the baby-sitting room. We become regulars, going every Monday, Wednesday, and Friday while Carrie is at camp. But while the break I get makes the day pass more quickly, swimming does not knit my life together here as it did in New Jersey. This pool is crowded and cold. I miss my lifeguard. My shoulders are looser, but my mind is still numb.

Before I started seeing Kate, nearly every therapist I saw scolded me for the same shortcoming: I don't let myself feel. During tough times, I have to remind myself of this problem. Usually that's all it takes: I remember my unhappiness must be the result of a submerged emotion, locate the feeling like a masseuse finding a knotted muscle, stroke it to the surface and experience its tenderness and dissipation. But this time it is hard to find the forgotten feeling. It's not day care or work. It's not a problem with Dave. So it must be . . . *I'm mourning my lost youth.*

When I announce this to Dave, I collapse on the bed and start to bawl.

"This is the end for us," I hiccup.

"What are you talking about?"

"We're not having any more kids, so we're done with all the big events. My whole life I've looked forward to the big events. First you graduate from high school, then college, then get married, buy a house, have babies. And you're the center of attention for all of them. But now we don't have any big events until Carrie's wedding. So, we're just in the background. All the big events will happen to the kids now and we'll just get old."

He looks at me as if I'm, well, you know.

"I just have to get over this," I tell him. "It's just something to get through."

I even tell a friend who's recently had her final child this ridiculous theory.

"Oh, I feel younger than ever with a new baby," she says.

We need something new in our lives, I decide, so that we don't feel so old and stagnant. A vacation. One cloudy Friday afternoon I open a guidebook to travel in New England, call country inns and bed and breakfasts and amusement parks for brochures and reservation rates, then prepare a list of options. I call Liz and ask if she and her family want to rent a late summer beach house with us. I ask another friend where she stays every year in Maine. In the end, though, it is impossible for me to make a decision between destinations. It's hard enough finding the perfect baby bottle.

Max is not having trouble with the bottles from which he drinks his breast milk, so I don't know why I think I need to improve on them. But every few weeks I switch styles and buy a whole supply of the latest. Plastic bag bottles that deflate like water balloons as they empty, just like mom's breast, the advertisement says. Hard plastic bottles bent like elbows or straight ones adorned with Dalmatians or clowns. Bottles with curly orthodontic nipples meant to look like the human counterpart. Straight, squared-off nipples. Four-ounce bottles. Eight-ounce bottles. I buy every variety except an antique glass bottle. The change, the newness, seems like a solution, as if anything new will make the old and bad go away.

But if bottles won't do it, maybe a new book will. The fat paperback with a Matisse-style painting of a vase of tulips on the front holds so many potential solutions I can't believe I haven't bought it sooner. There are chapters on changing negative thoughts to positive ones, on learning to relax through deep breathing and repetition of a soothing word, on exercising the world away, on good sleep hygiene. I try them all. I stay away from the bed unless I'm there to sleep and make sure the room is airy and dark. I take my walks and swim my laps. I try deep breathing with a special word, but cannot decide between peace and sleep. I try to put a positive spin on exhaustion.

Such solutions might work for a normally stressed person. But not for someone whose other strategy for recovery involves smelling seashells before bed.

We've gone to the beach once this summer. We visited college friends of Dave—two women and their babies and toddlers—who were renting a house overlooking Narragansett Bay on the rim of Rhode Island. I told the women I was having trouble sleeping and they invited me to stay at the beach with them. I knew if I had stayed, inhaling moist salt air and hearing the ocean breathe all night, I would have slept soundly. But Dave had to work the next day, so we left at dusk. At home, I put one of the ashtray-size white clamshells the kids had collected on my night table. It smells of the beach. It reminds me of those nurturing young mothers who offered me a bed. I hold it to my nose and inhale every night before bed, as if smelling the sea will bring me there, and being there will cure me. Then I tell my problems to six tiny worry dolls made of bright thread wound around wire. According to some Guatemalan legend, they are supposed to solve problems overnight and take on the responsibility of worrying. I squeeze them between my fingers and rub my worries into them like prayers. Help me sleep. Help me take care of my kids. Help me relax. Help me stop worrying. Help me find myself under all this mess.

M aybe a day to myself will help to unearth the old me. Normally, a train ride to Boston and a day of reading in restaurants and shopping for clothes will sand away my stress. Since it is summer, I decide to take the day to myself in Marblehead. Nosing into the sea of Massachusetts's north shore, Marblehead is home to beaches and yacht clubs, two centuries old Federal Colonials that sit close to the road and waterfront mansions that keep watch over the Atlantic. It was also once home to me, when I worked for two years writing about school board meetings and wealthy sailors for the *Marblehead Reporter*. I lived in a bad apartment on a dead-end street where I stayed home alone at night fighting over the phone with my long-distance boyfriend. But I loved the curving antique streets and the smell of the fishing boats and the thick chowder from a restaurant called the Barnacle. I know a day there will soothe me.

I stop at the bakery that makes my favorite cinnamon sugar cookies. I browse in the used bookstore owned by a young man and an older woman who share a passion for each other and book-buying trips to Britain. At the Barnacle, I sit by the window that overlooks the harbor and eat chowder with a thick stream of butter and sprinkles of paprika floating over the cream. I feel good. This trip is doing the trick, I think. Then I head into a clothing boutique and am stopped in my tracks by an anxiety attack. I sweat. My stomach cramps. I berate myself for letting myself get anxious during such an idyllic day. Then I search for reasons, remembering to feel. Maybe a longing for my single days has hit suddenly. Maybe being so close to the house where my work friend Kenny used to live, where I learned to drive a stick shift on his Saab with the hole rusted in the floor, and where we spent lunch breaks eating canned soup and watching cartoons has made me miss him so intensely that the feelings backed up and turned into anxiety. Finally, as I am sitting on the curb outside the store, the anxiety fades, only to be replaced by deep sadness. It starts to rain. I sit on a bench at the beach and watch the charcoal sea beat at the course sand. I reach into my bag and pull out a tiny spiral notebook, start to write self-pitying poetry. The poems are all directed at Max.

I sit by the ocean
Where I belong
And think of you
To whom I belong
And wonder
How will I ever make this work?
When will I stop feeling choked?
When will my love for you equal my anger?

At the end of that failed adventure, I begin to admit that maybe I can't fix myself. But that still doesn't mean I have a mental illness. There is still the possibility that all this craziness is linked to a purely physical root. Postpartum thyroiditis, a disorder of the thyroid gland that is fairly common after pregnancy, can cause depression. I was treated for a low thyroid throughout my pregnancy. If I have an imbalance, a few thyroid pills should patch me right up.

I head back to the doctor who told me to take a vacation so I can get a thyroid blood test. It is early morning, before camp, and I have both kids with me. I park them in the hallway outside the blood room and take a seat. A nurse wraps a rubber ribbon around my biceps until the thick green cord of a vein rises under my skin. She swabs the inside of my elbow with alcohol, then sticks a needle in a test tube.

"Make a fist," she says.

I look away. I hate to see the needle pierce my thin, white skin. I turn back when she pulls off the rubber strip, which sets my blood gushing from the pressure release. I watch the purple blood fill up the tube and pray it contains evidence. *Come on thyroid problems,* I think, wishing my rounded fist contained a set of dice and that this was all a game.

"Unclench your fist."

Needle out. Gauze and bandage on. Tube of blood shaken, labeled, and placed in a partitioned box that looks like a miniature of the ones milkmen used to leave on front steps. Eight hours later I call for the results.

"Everything's fine," the receptionist tells me. "Your thyroid's normal."

It must be obvious to Kate that none of my strategies is working. Besides seeing her twice a week, I call every few days with neurotic questions. She has given me her emergency number and told me to call at any time with any question. I don't hesitate.

"My fingers have been tingling," I tell her one early morning over the phone. "Is that because of the Klonopin?"

No, she explains patiently, I'm probably just hyperventilating and not getting enough oxygen to my extremities. Try deep breathing.

Another time: "I took a quarter of a Klonopin and it didn't work. Should I go up to a half?"

"Sure, why don't you try that."

"You don't think it's too much? You think I'll be okay?"

Half a yellow tablet starts to tame the insomnia. The extra sleep gives me more energy with which to worry.

People suffering from obsessiveness should be spared the informational inserts that come with prescription medicine. The Klonopin insert, as thin and crinkly as ancient parchment, tells me that the drug could be habit forming and should be used with caution. I add to the merry-go-round of thoughts in my head the fear that I will become an addict. I will never be able to get clean. I will never be able to fall asleep by myself. I will end up in detox.

I save my Zoloft questions for our appointments. They consist mostly of me interrogating Kate about antidepressants, in general.

"How do you know I need it? What will it do to me? How does it work on the brain? How do you know this is the right one for me?" I ask.

She tells me my physical symptoms indicate that I'm clinically depressed and that the drug will be effective. She explains the limited knowledge anyone has about how SSRI antidepressants work. Depressed people have a shortage of a neurotransmitter called serotonin, which is thought to be responsible for emotional well-being. Selective serotonin reuptake inhibitors prevent the reabsorption of serotonin, so there's an ample supply of the stuff. She tells me she often prescribes Zoloft to anxious people rather than its celebrity cousin, Prozac, because Prozac can bring on more anxiety.

By themselves, asking these questions is not unreasonable. Every patient has a right to know about the cure being held out to her. But I ask them again and again and again, consulting a wrinkled piece of notebook paper that I scrawl notes on between visits.

"What will happen if I don't take it?"

"If you don't take it," she says, sighing, "you'll feel better, too, but it will take a lot longer. And it be will harder to deal with your problems. It's like you're carrying a big weight now. If you took the medication, that weight would be gone."

To ease my concern that she is withholding information from me, she gives me a photocopy of the adverse affects of SSRIs. Kate's handout only helps to add another horse to my carousel of obsessions: suicide. *Precipitation of hypomania or mania, psychosis, panic reactions, anxiety, or euphoria may occur; isolated reports of antidepressants causing agitation, impulsivity, and suicidal urges.* Not what I need to read thirty-seven times a day. And so another excuse not to accept the help I need.

With the few minutes remaining in my therapy appointments after I've asked my drug questions, we talk about my problems. During one session, she tells me she thinks I'm experiencing a kind of post-traumatic stress disorder. Like war veterans and rape victims, I'm awash in raw emotions I've suppressed for two years. It happens when we're safe, she explains. In my case, I'm free of worrying about dying babies, so now all the pain of losing two fetuses and holding desperately on to one is flushing itself out.

Kate also explains that until I straighten out my brain's

wiring deficiencies with antidepressants, I won't have the perspective and clarity needed to grasp problem-solving skills. When your brain is always battling itself, there's hardly any energy left for common sense. But I can't understand that at the time. I only feel incompetent and deeply ashamed about my dependence on therapy. It is more proof, I am sure, of my failure as a person.

Later, Kate and I will work on my self-esteem and the problems I've always had with perfectionism, among other things. With a clear brain, it will finally be easier to get to the bottom of my issues, to see the traps I've set for myself all my life. And Kate, my eighth therapist, will sit more quietly than any of the others. She will not use her tools to repair my life, as the others have. She will wait, watching, as I pick up my own hammer and chisel and start the renovation myself.

But first I must get myself that new brain. I'm not ready yet.

I still turn to my pink PPD self-help book almost daily. *This Isn't What I Expected* by Kleiman and Raskin isn't the intimate companion I had hoped for, but reading summaries of other women's lives during PPD makes me feel less alone. And the factual information supplied by the psychiatrist and social worker who wrote it usually pushes me forward. The voices of these faceless authority figures are both encouraging and sympathetic.

Denial is the paste that keeps the PPD sufferer from instantly crumbling when she is diagnosed, the book tells me. It's is a very common "almost knee-jerk reaction." Many of us can accept the diagnoses intellectually, but not emotionally. It's the stigma of mental illness that hangs us up. So we continue to lie to ourselves and others. Sure, we say, we've got this PPD thing, but don't worry, we'll snap out of it soon. This lie can even be helpful at first, Kleiman and Raskin write.

"Denial is what makes it possible for you to continue to do

the things you don't feel like doing, such as cleaning the house, going to work, getting the children dressed. But when denial is carried too far, the mechanism that originally set out to protect you backfires and can delay the healing process."

Bingo.

The irregularity of PPD can also feed denial. Like the roller coaster of moods that can possess me during a single day, there are also high and low days. Once in a while I feel absolutely fine. I have fun, sleep normally, think clearly for a whole day. And I convince myself I can't possibly be ill. "See," I say to Dave, "I don't need drugs. I'm just a little stressed." Then, with no pattern and no warning at all, a string of lousy days returns. But because I remember the high, I blame the low on myself. I must not be coping well with something. I must not be trying hard enough. I will fix this myself.

The minutes before my husband comes home to relieve me of the kids have always been the longest for me. Now, they are unbearable. One evening in mid-August, I cling to the edge of the butcher-block kitchen table as if it were the only thing anchoring me to the earth. Carrie watches a video and Max sways in his baby swing. I am having the scariest anxiety attack of the summer so far. It came out of nowhere. There is no one here to make me feel suffocated, no day care to worry about, not even much insomnia anymore. Yet I can't stop shaking or sweating, and I want to cry out for help, as if a real threat were approaching.

When Dave comes home, the attack is still going strong. Usually they only last a few minutes. I tell him about it, then cry as he eats his dinner. When he's done, I drive across town to Kelly's house. We've made plans to go for a walk together.

She walks briskly, getting a real workout from her nightly strolls. The speed helps to calm me, the perspiring lets the anxiety seep from my pores. I ask her what she thinks about antidepressants.

"Would you take them?" I say as we round the corner that leads to her house.

"I would if the depression was ongoing," she says, "if no matter what I tried, I didn't feel better."

She has just described me. I look up at the beautiful homes in her neighborhood, the purple and yellow Victorian, and the narrow century-old Colonials. I'm not sure where we are, but I feel comforted here. Many generations have lived in these houses, men and women who suffered and rejoiced, who cried and shook and tried to walk off their troubles. And then I say it: Uncle. The wrestling match between my ego and a bottle of tiny lavender pills is over. The next day I fill my first prescription for Zoloft.

Chapter 5

The bottle of pills sits on my dresser, teasing me. I shake a few of the purple ovals into my palm, a fistful of fallen flower petals, and examine them. They are delicate and lovely, monogrammed with their name and weight. I wonder how they could possibly possess any power. I can't discover how potent they are yet because I am not to let one touch my tongue until I have weaned Max. Still, just glimpsing the plastic cylinder that houses them anchors me somewhat. The pills are something new to hold on to, a floatation device or the steel edge of the pool. For most of my thirty-two years, I have been holding on, knowing that if I let go, if I fall into the ocean of depression that has always stirred below me, I will drown. Since Max's birth, my grip has weakened considerably. But I have not let go so far, nor do I plan to. Those pills, that bottle: I will white-knuckle them until I am well again.

But first I must lose my son.

I have already cut down to about three breastfeedings a day. The nursing experts recommend dropping a feeding every one to two weeks so the body and the baby can adjust. But there's no time for that. So, every few days I substitute bottle for breast until there is only one nursing session left. I sit with him at nightfall in a white rocking chair that glides. He lies in my arms and smiles up at me. *Let's start,* his face says, *this is our time. Let's end,* I think, *this is the last time.* I pull up the flap of my royal blue nursing shirt, which I wear several times a week and which I will never need again. Underneath, a plump breast encased in white lace pokes through a slit in the blue fabric. I unsnap the bra at my breastbone and cup the breast in my left hand. My right hand holds Max's silky skull. His lips wrap around my nipple and milk drips down from its sealed cartons like pinpricks in my chest. He reaches up and places a hand on the fat, white veiny flesh of my breast, a tiny butterfly on a dinosaur's egg. He looks me in the eyes: blue to green, bright to weary.

This nursing relationship is the only thing that has gone well for me in Max's life. While my nursing bond with Carrie was a seven-month wrestling match, my experience with Max has been a waltz. We fit. It is that chemistry again, same with same melding into one. It is intimacy, the sweetest of codependent relationships. No one else in our family knows what it feels like to do this. It is our secret, our ritual. He is part of me still, as when he lived under my heart and beside my liver. I am the reason he thrives, and the only one who can give him the natural elixir that keeps him alive. He is the only one who can relieve the pain the fullness of milk brings, the only one who can start the wash of hormones that soothe like a shot of Jack Daniels when the milk starts flowing. As long as we are nursing, he is dependent and trusting and I am capable and giving. When we stop, someone else will keep him thriving. He will transfer his trust and I will lose my place at the top of his list, for many months.

I hate doing this to him. Neither of us is ready. He is only five months old. I had hoped to nurse him until he was one. I feel as if I'm abandoning him without explanation, blowing off my best junior high friend without leaving a note on her locker. It will hurt us both, as if that cruel labor and delivery nurse had cut the umbilical cord before he emerged from my body. I am not one of those women who loves the act of breastfeeding. I find it messy, time-consuming, exhausting, and confining. But I love the closeness of the nursing relationship. Later, when I am better and I see a woman nursing, my dry breasts will tingle still. And Max, even when he is a toddler, will plunge his hand into my bra when he is nervous. People will stare as he gropes my breast.

"I guess I didn't nurse him for long enough," I tell them, as I smile over the wince of memory.

When he finishes with this last nursing, I wipe the milk from the corner of his lips and from the tip of my breast with a cloth diaper. I snap the bra, pull down the flap of the shirt, lift Max to my shoulder, and stand. He burps once, twice, then I lay him in his crib to sleep. I wind the mobile above his head and it tings out the notes to "My Favorite Things."

It takes two days for the tears to arrive. They come masked in another sorrow. I am marching on and off a jade-green plastic step in an aerobics class when I think about our cat, Simon. He is a big, orange hairball who causes my husband to wheeze. To spare Dave's lungs, we've tried to segregate man from beast. First Simon was banned from our bed, then the top floor, then the house. Now he sleeps on a towel in a gift box in the garage. But we know it is too cold for him to sleep there in the winter, so we've found a new home for him. He will move out over Labor Day weekend to live with a family who takes in foster children and pets. They live in an old house that backs up to an Audubon bird sanctuary property. He will live there for three months before he is killed by a speeding car.

I think of losing Simon, whom I love almost as much as my children, and I start to cry. I can't stop. I keep doing my clumsy step exercises, but I can't stop weeping. When the music stops, I leave my step in the middle of the floor and run to my car. It is a child's cry I emit, an uncensored wail. Once in the car, my grief shifts from Simon to Max. He's drifting from me, too, and that's so much worse than the cat. Without nursing, I will never be as close to my baby again. I am losing something I had no intention of giving up, losing it because my body has failed me again. My brain went this time instead of my thyroid or uterus, the two parts that malfunctioned when I was pregnant or trying to conceive. Then my sorrow spins into rage, like one song that segues to another in a medley. I pound the steering wheel, glimpsing out the windows first to make sure no one's looking. I cry and pound until I see the aerobics teacher walk toward her car. Then I drive away.

Once I stop nursing Max, there is no need for me to answer his cries in the night, so I lose him some more. Armed with a bottle from the fridge, Dave can be his lifeline now. And I have no excuse for not sleeping through the night. Kate has insisted I do everything possible to get solid nights of sleep. Dave agrees that this is essential to my recovery. Though he skips work more often than he should, comes home early when my voice weakens on the phone and listens to me catalog my symptoms, helping me to sleep is the most concrete contribution Dave can make to my survival. Discovering this task helps him, too. He is no longer resigned to the bleachers to watch me strike out. He has found his purpose, like a visiting great-aunt who polishes all the silver.

The first step in the sleeping program is for Dave, whose nocturnal growls and snorts have always woken me in the middle of the night, to move to the pull-out couch in the living room. The second is to drown out any potentially disturbing sounds that could sneak under the closed bedroom door. A loud fan is placed in the window by the bed even though we have central air conditioning. The fan serves as white noise to muffle any cries from Max that may break through my Klonopin-induced sleep. It is very quiet in the room, and very lonely without my loud, strong human security blanket sleeping next to me. Instead of his hand, I clutch Pinky, the blanket given to me at birth. It's a small square of white waffley thermal material rimmed in pink satin. I spent my childhood nights picking at with my fingernails until I fell asleep. When I ripped the satin from the blanket, my grandmother would sew it back on by hand in wide stitches. I brought Pinky to college, gave a corner of it to a scared man I once loved, and keep it in a top drawer of my dresser in case I need it. Once or twice a year I wrap it around my belly when I have a bad stomachache. It always works, tempering my pain and putting me to sleep. And it helps pacify me now, though I worry that I'll use up all its magic by clinging to it nightly.

One day Dave brings home a sound machine that plays the voices of nature. It's from Brookstone, a store that sells very expensive gadgets.

"How much was it?" I ask, knowing there isn't a line item in our budget for gadgets.

"A lot," he says. "But don't worry. If it helps you sleep, it's worth it."

With the touch of a button the gray box becomes a babbling brook, waves hitting a beach, rain, wind, streams. I sit alone on our king-size bed, all but padlocked into the bedroom, and choose the beach. I imagine it'll be just like sleeping on a mat on the sand. The waves sound as crisp and clear as waves would sound if every other noise on earth were silenced. This immediately short-circuits the fantasy. Maybe somewhere there is an ocean that slaps the earth without being diluted by other sounds of life. But without wind, screaming children, lifeguard whistles, or squawking seagulls, it doesn't feel like the beach to me. I switch to rain and try to fall asleep to that for a few nights. But it too sounds artificially crisp. I feel like the windowpane the rain hits instead of the ear that hears it drop. I hug Dave and tell him to take his expensive gift back to the store. It cost $200. The fan works better.

But just in case I can still hear Max wake in the night, Dave packs him up and moves him to the living room, too. He sleeps in an uncomfortable portable crib next to his dad's uncomfortable couch, two guys roughing it as if on a fishing trip. When he wakes at night, Dave gives him a bottle and sings him the Mockingbird song until he falls back to sleep. Eventually, Dave will teach Max to give up the midnight snack completely and sleep through the night. I had fantasized since pregnancy of the morning I would wake up after a full night's sleep and realize the baby had slept through the night and that normal life had begun again. I would open my eyes and see on the clock a healthy morning hour: seven A.M. or eight even. Then there would be a moment of panic: What happened to the baby? He didn't wake me at all—he must be dead! Finally, a long moment of victory: Yes! Through the night. An event worthy of a cheer. Two, four, six, eight. What do we appreciate? Sleep, sleep, sleeping through the night!

That scenario would have meant I had survived the whole exhausting infancy stage and could now enjoy motherhood. But I never have that morning. My husband has it. My husband gets my baby to sleep through the night, patting Max's tiny back for reassurance as he learns to cry himself to sleep, then to chew his blanket until he's sleeping again. My husband gets to see the baby's eyes close and his face soften as he pulls formula from a bottle with his tongue. And when Max wakes before dawn, my husband gets to carry him still warm from sleep into his bed, curling with him in the spoon position, serving spoon against demitasse, the baby's heart beating against his. My husband. Not me. I am upstairs, alone. I have abandoned my baby and he no longer needs me.

I mother Max differently after our physical relationship ends. I still take care of him, but I am not present. I feed him and I change his diapers when I am supposed to. I go through the motions of making homemade peach baby food, but hate the chore. With Carrie, steaming slices of peaches, pears, zucchini, or chunks of carrots and chicken, then spinning them to a pulp in a spice grinder was a joy. I was an earth mother! I was sparing my baby from living on processed food. But with Max it is all work: fruit dripping on the countertops, grinder to wash by hand, dollops of food to freeze in ice cube trays. I do it once, then lower my standards. Jars of fruit are good enough.

I am sure Max senses my absence. Babies sense everything. If there's tension in the house, they cry more. If you're sad, they'll cuddle. And while he never stops grinning, he must wonder where his mother, once rich in milk and tenderness, has gone. *Where is the one who loved me so well?* he may think. *And who is this sack of bones moving me from place to place without eye contact?*

L etting go of Max is the biggest loss so far, but it frees my hands to seize my cure. I can finally start taking the Zoloft. *Now* I will be okay, I think, and this awful intrusion in my life will end. I've made this concession to the gods of control: *okay, okay,* I've said, *I can't control everything.* I admit that I need some help from biotechnology, that I am unable to fix my brain by myself. But in a couple of weeks, when the pills fix me up, I'll be all right again. I will be in charge again. This is what I think.

It takes about two weeks for antidepressants to work, according to Kate, the paragraphs in books I read over and over, and the insert the pharmacist tucks into the narrow white bag that hides my pills. Two weeks. Three hundred and thirty-six hours. Twenty thousand, one hundred, and sixty minutes. And I feel nearly all of them, waiting, waiting, for this miracle drug to work. A Depression After Delivery spokeswoman I've talked to on the phone tells me Prozac worked so quickly for her that she was singing to songs on the car radio two days after starting it. I press the buttons that bounce the reception from station to station and song to song on the radio in my van, but I have no urge to harmonize with the rock stars.

I take my first Zoloft on a hot Saturday at the beginning of August. The highest recommended dose is 200 milligrams. I start at twelve and a half, one quarter of the smallest pill made. Kate has told me to start on the weekend when Dave is home in case the pills make me drowsy and unable to care for the kids. I'm not drowsy, but I feel slightly dizzy the first time I drive. Later, there is a mild headache, but those side effects go away by the end of the first day. On Sunday after dinner, I sit on a beach chair on my front lawn reading a book. *Reading* a book, not just looking at the same sentence until I give up. Carrie walks out of the screen door and I rise out of my chair to play tag with her among the boulders and trees of our front yard. She squeals as I chase her, and I laugh out loud as she chases me back, her arms spread in front of her as she tries to reach her distant mother. When she goes inside for a bath, I stay outside until day turns to dusk. Then I notice it: silence. Not from the outside, but from the inside. My head is quiet, my breathing relaxed. A flash of my old self rises to the surface. The me who is not terrified of the words in her head or the world outside her body. The me who smiles at the thought of playing with her daughter and whose chest billows with love for the girl. *Hey, I remember you,* I think. But the image is only a spark that burns out by bedtime.

Two days later, the old stable me nudges past the new sick me again as I am sitting in Kate's office. It is quiet again and I feel cleansed, as I did on my front lawn. At the end of the session, as she walks me to her door, I give her a hug.

"It worked!" I tell her. "Thank you!"

"Oh, Susan, I'm so glad," she says, and I'm never sure whether she's just playing along or really thinks I've recovered by essentially breathing in the dust of Zoloft tablets. *I* believe I am well because of those two forays into tranquillity. As it turns out, they are only previews of a movie that won't be released for months. These parties at which I mingle with my old self happen just often enough to lure me forward, but not so often that I declare a miraculous recovery again.

Two weeks after taking the first pill, when there is still no singing to be heard in my car, I complain to Kate.

"Maybe these aren't right for me," I say. "Maybe I need something different."

I've read about Prozac. I want Prozac. But Kate doesn't like prescribing it. She says it can exacerbate anxiety and insomnia, and that it has a long half-life, so if I needed to switch to another pill I'd have to go cold turkey for a while. She prefers Zoloft for women, she says. So I stick with it, this Lady Schick of antidepressants.

"Sometimes it takes three or four weeks," she says now.

At four weeks and with only the subtlest improvement, I am again given a two-week deadline to cling to.

"It can take up to six weeks," Kate tells me that day.

I realize then that the whole two-week promise is just a party line cooked up by the medical establishment to keep us patients hanging on until the drug really works. Those charged with getting us well have to lie a little because they know us. If we were told it would take six weeks to get better, an interminable time for the feeble of mind, many of us would opt for the razor blade, the shotgun, the fistful of sleeping pills. So they keep from us the real story, which is that it takes two weeks to get better all right, but you can't start counting until you reach your therapeutic dose. That's the amount that your particular brain needs to start maintaining an ample seratonin stock. It varies with everyone, which is why patients start with a standard dose of antidepressants and gradually take more or less until the right balance is reached. And it takes me seven weeks to get to my therapeutic dose.

This is my fault, or the fault of my diseased brain, for I am too scared of the potential side effects of the pills to take enough to help me. Kate doesn't push for me to take more than I'm ready for, but she gently suggests that the more medication I take the sooner I'll get better. It is an irony suffered by so many of the mentally ill: our illnesses make us too skittish to devour what will make us well. For now, the battle march of the drug is too faint and slow to drive the depression away.

My magic number of Zoloft milligrams will be 150. I will reach it by slowly increasing the amount of pill I put in my mouth and decreasing the amount I drop back in the bottle. I slice them with a blue plastic tool that looks like a stapler but has a razor blade wedged in the middle. Sometimes the cut is clean. Other times, tiny crumbs of purple dust linger on the counter. I lick my fingertip and scoop the particles up so that I am ingesting exactly the amount of drug I intend to take that week. First I go up to 25 milligrams, then 50 and 75. At 100 milligrams I graduate to the peach-colored pills and then start chopping them into fractions. I will finally reach 150 at the end of September, more than six months after Max's birth.

But my recovery is not as simple as that. It is not just a math equation: Add pills, subtract depression, problem solved. First, I must sink to the bottom of the ocean floor.

I flick through the cable channels one night and see the analogy swim across my television screen. It is a nature show, filmed underwater, and watching it makes me feel as if I've been holding my breath for too long. The narrator explains the procreation of squid. The mother squid plants a tubelike sack of eggs in the sand on the ocean floor before sinking to the bottom to die. Her job is done. She has brought new life into the world, and must now surrender her own vitality. This is exactly how I feel. Max is thriving. I am dying.

This day, like all the others during August, has been like one long fingernail scratch on a blackboard. Every moment hurts. Even with the Zoloft busily multiplying my seratonin population, I am almost constantly in pain. There is a never-ending feeling of agitation, like layers of grime that can't be washed off or an itchy wool turtleneck clamped around the neck. Everything—answering a child's question, untucking a shirt to go to the bathroom, thinking of what to have for lunch—takes so much effort. Too much effort.

This morning I woke up to a familiar sensation: dread seeping through my body, my heart throbbing unsteadily. I do not want to face any of these days, but I don't want to stay in bed either. That would mean being alone. I walk down the stairs and see Dave feeding the kids. Carrie sits at the table eating a bagel and Max sits in his high chair. Dave, with a dishtowel around his neck to protect his shirt and tie from splashes of baby food, spoons rice cereal into Max's face. I am safe for a few more minutes, until Dave has to drive to the train station. I watch the clock. He leaves at 7:45. It is 7:22.

I microwave a cup of decaf tea and sit on the couch. *Sesame Street* is on. But even this isn't safe. I fill with hatred whenever an adult appears on screen. *How come you're so happy?* I think. *How come your life with kids looks so easy?* Even the Muppets annoy me, with their vibrant colors and high-pitched voices. Bright light and loud noise have started to overwhelm me, as if my brain can't process such sensations.

"What are you doing today?" Dave asks.

"I don't know."

"It's nice out. Why don't you go to the lake?"

Is he kidding me? Although I am desperate for a break from motherhood, my responsibilities doubled last week. For most of the summer, I have had the burden of taking care of only one child while Carrie was at camp. I have had one hour to myself three times a week when I put Max in the Jewish Community Center baby-sitting room. But now camp is over and the baby-sitting room doesn't allow children as old as Carrie. I am stuck at home with no structure, no breaks, and no help. And he wants me to schlep them to the lake?

I can't justify hiring a baby-sitter when I'm not working. It's part punishment—you're too weak to work, so you don't deserve a break; part bravado—if other women can mother two kids without help, so can you. Also, there's the money. Last year our accountant forgot to tell us that when Dave became a partner at his law firm, we had to pay self-employment taxes. Oops, forgot to mention it. So we owed tens of thousands of dollars at tax time in April. We had to empty our savings accounts and borrow from the law firm and now we're trying to be as frugal as humanly possible. We buy cheap drugstore brand diapers and eat generic macaroni and cheese. A splurge is a trip to the farm stand for fresh corn on the cob at forty cents an ear. Wasting the day at the mall is out of the question.

Pepper still isn't well enough to come up and baby-sit. She walks with a cane now and is too weak to drive by herself or to carry a baby. And my mother has twisted a muscle and dislodged a vertebra in her back. A doctor tells her she could be paralyzed if she walks before she's healed, so she is confined to bed for the rest of the summer. I don't expect her to take care of the kids in that condition, but I want her to come keep me company so I won't have to be alone with them.

"Just have Dad drive you up," I say one afternoon. "Lie down in the back of the car all the way, and when you get here you can stay on the couch the whole time."

I am begging, demanding, but she cannot deliver. All she can do is mail me a check so I can pay for hired help.

The Depression After Delivery people can't sit by my side either. The support group takes the summer off and won't start meeting again until after Labor Day. I dream daily of sitting around a conference table with women who've survived this: strong, kind women who will promise I'll make it out alive, too. I call Karen, my DAD contact, and ask for a phone buddy in the interim. Though my friend Liz understands how it feels to have PPD, she recovered before having to resort to drugs. I want to connect with someone who's had as severe a case as I do. Just a PPD survivor who will listen and reassure me until the support group starts. But she never calls me with a name.

"We'll find something to do," I tell Dave, as he exchanges dishtowel for suitcoat and grabs his briefcase. He kisses us, then leaves and when the door closes behind him I stand at the window watching his car back out of the driveway. Then he's gone and I am in charge.

I sit at the kitchen table with a bowl of Kix and flip through the *Times* and the *Globe*. Like an illiterate, I turn the pages and look at the pictures. Sometimes I read the first paragraph of an article, but I never finish or retain it. After eating, I start to unload the dishwasher. Then I remember there is laundry to do. I bring down a basket of clothes and leave it on top of the washer. I return to the dishes, but before I finish, I spot the nursery school bill on the counter. It is due today, so I set out to pay it, a colossal task involving numbers and stamps. It is ten o'clock now and time for Max's nap. Carrie, thankfully, could watch TV all day. I leave her in front of a show with ethnically diverse puppets while I take Max upstairs for his bottle.

Between the busywork of naps, meals, and housework, I manage to pass a good chunk of the day. But after Max wakes up in the afternoon, the hardest part starts. I am nervous when I count the remaining hours. It is 3:30. Dave drives up at 6:20. I am jittery and tired, like someone recovering from an adrenaline rush. Three hours. Three hours. What do I do with these kids?

I spread an old blanket on the front lawn and sprinkle it with toys. Carrie builds villages with blocks. Max chews on stuffed animals. I sit next to them, waiting. Waiting for a car to drive by, which never happens. Waiting for someone, anyone, to walk by. Waiting for the clock to strike dinnertime.

I plunk Carrie in front of a video and preheat the oven. Then I settle into a chair in the living room to give Max another bottle. When he finishes, I carry him into the kitchen. I walk by the hot oven and it menaces me, as it has many times this summer. I imagine it snapping open its jaws and threatening to gobble him in. But not by its own power. I don't see the oven taking the baby. I see something worse in the images that flash by my eyes: the mother giving the baby to the oven. Kelly tells me one day that she heard at a conference that women hospitalized with postpartum psychiatric illnesses share a common fear: that they will put their babies in the microwave. I have the same fear of the oven. When I walk by it holding Max and it is hot, I get a feeling of terror that I will suddenly lose control of myself and shove him in. I don't want to hurt him in any way. The thought of cooking him paints my upper lip with cold sweat. But he is the size of a roasting chicken and I believe I have no control of anything. I have lost this much control of myself, what if I go one step further and become a murderer? What if my brain slips down a rung from depressed to psychotic? If an oven and a baby could come together in my mind, what else am I capable of?

I put him in his saucer and shut off the oven. We'll get Chinese instead. I return to the living room chair alone and cry until the shaking stops. Then Dave comes home and takes over, keeping his children safe from their mother. And I fade from their lives for the rest of the night, like the mother squid I later watch on TV.

B esides eating and napping, I don't remember what the kids and I do with ourselves most of the days. Time is blurred. Later, I will remember the details of the activities that filled the months before and after this one quite clearly. But these weeks of getting sicker before I get better fade like sun-bleached drapes, never to be displayed in sharp colors again.

The images that fill my head will never fade, though. I had thought I was experiencing the darkest of night before I started taking the Zoloft. But there must have been a nightlight on somewhere. Before the day really begins again, the nightlight is finally snapped off and pure black envelops me. The darkness manifests itself in terrifying pictures projected onto my imagination.

My once fine brain has been chopped in half with a hatchet. Inside, it is filled with mashed watermelon pulp, black seeds floating down mealy pink rivers. Later, as I heal, I imagine there is a zipper attached to the two halves of melon, the teeth meeting gradually to make me whole again. Or my head is a can of worms, opened with the sharp disk of a can opener. Or I am made of layers. The real me is buried deep inside under a thick coiled strip of cotton, the kind that covers vitamins in a new bottle. I think rational thoughts once in a while, but they usually can't permeate the covering. Until the cotton is removed, the stable me will be out of reach. Instead, the world will see the outer layer, a brittle woman going through the motions of living, barely human at all. And between those two layers is the me I fear the most.

For four years of college, and a couple after that, I hung a poster of François Truffaut's movie *The Wild Child* on the back of my bedroom door. I'd bought it at the bookstore, attracted, I suppose, to the raw emotion in the drawing depicted on it. It is a head-and-shoulders portrait of a boy raised by wolves—a filthy, naked human with long, unruly hair, his mouth opened in a howl. He is painted in the yellow, orange, and brown tones of fire. The poster became a joke among my close friends because I would mess up my hair and distort my face in an imitation of The Wild Child. I could pretend to become him, ha ha. But now I feel that I have. He is inside me, that untamed creature, jerking with fear, screaming in pain, frightening himself and the world, ready to chew off his own foot. I can't tame him or control him. He lets out yelps of uncensored thoughts, words, phrases. *Death, mental hospital, sleep, bad mother, incompetent,* he screams at me. His noise drowns out the quiet, whole me stuffed under the cotton.

Having clinical depression, which is what PPD is, is like having no censor for thoughts or emotions. Everything that comes up—things that usually get caught in the net of the subconscious and dealt with in dreams—comes to the surface shimmering with energy. They are urgent, insistent, impossible to ignore. Impulses. Obsessions. Without its seratonin lubrication, the mind can't stop thoughts from going around and around. They're a whirlpool of water that can't go down the drain. A depressed mind also has no quality control. Any old fear or hurt, anger or regret, gets magnified and thrust forward. It is not sorted and put away, classified as irrational or past. There are no more defense mechanisms to shield one from the barbs of feelings. The brain is too tired to employ them, too tired to oversee much beyond breathing and heartbeat, so everything comes to the surface.

Impulses a healthy mind would never have to deal with become real. Like the oven. Or the slate floor at the bottom of the
stairs, which once invited me to throw Max down. These split-
second horror flicks are followed by tremendous slaps of guilt.
What kind of awful person would think that, I yell at myself in my
head, *you should be ashamed.* And I am. The shame is so deep that
I can't tell anyone about these thoughts, not Kate and especially not
Dave. He still thinks I'm a good mother. All I can do is bat the images away, put the baby down and leave the kitchen or hold tight to
him as I walk down the stairs. Fortunately, someone is always in the
house with me when those thoughts invade. But I wonder what I
would do if I was all alone with Max. I try not to let that happen,
just in case.

I am afraid to be alone with myself, too, because suicide is
another of the thoughts I can't put back on a shelf. I have gone from
fearing that the pills will make me suicidal to obsessing over
whether I am. The knives on the kitchen counter threaten me.
Smooth black handles and long silver blades buried in the bosom of
a blond block of wood. Bread knife, carving knife, fish knife, par-
ing knife, chef's knife, suicide knife. One book I read says in bold
print that if you are feeling suicidal you should get to an emergency
room immediately. The unwritten words, of course, are that you
will then be admitted to a mental hospital and branded forever. So
I ask myself, *Am I feeling suicidal?* And I can't answer for sure. The
word, *suicide,* bounces around my head like a Ping-Pong ball,
jumping into my vision at unexpected times, every day. It is not followed or preceded by anything. No *I want to commit* at the beginning, no *seems like the only answer* at the end. I don't want to leave
this world. Quite the contrary: I want to rejoin the world and start
having fun. But that word, *suicide,* it's there again and again, just
another dirty word neglected by the vacationing censor in my
brain. I think of an evil gnome living in my head. *You have no de-
fenses against me,* it taunts, *I could rise up and get you at any time.*
I cower from him and from his ugly word. Suicide. Go away, I im-

plore. Stop thinking that. But I can't. The word spins and spins, searching for the drain. Maybe I am feeling suicidal. Maybe I should be hospitalized.

But no. Not that. Anything but that. I will later wonder whether my recovery would have been easier if I had been in a psychiatric ward. When I allow myself to consider it, going to the hospital seems soothing and ivory-colored, like a satin pillow. But the luxury of rest would have cost me too much, so I hold tight to the few strands of sanity I have left in order to avoid it. Before Max was born, my one easy success in life was motherhood. I was so good at it with Carrie, so competent. And now, I can do nothing with my children but park them in front of the television on warm summer afternoons. I cannot even comfort my baby in the night with my breast. Failing at motherhood completely is more than I can bear. If I keep taking care of them, if I'm here in body every day, I am still an adequate mother. If I have to let nurses take care of me, and their father take care of them, I will surrender my only success. So I don't let it happen. The flaw that has made my life so difficult—the psychic beatings I give myself, the breaks I never allow myself—works in my favor this time. "You would never treat anybody else as badly as you treat yourself," my friend Lauren told me in college. Others, I would have put to bed with tea and *I Love Lucy* reruns. Me, I don't stop. And it keeps me out of the hospital. Masochism wins over need.

So I get out of bed every morning, take a shower, and put on my makeup: creamy tan liquid on the soft puffy skin under my eyes, powdery rose particles on my protruding cheekbones, black paste on my lashes after I curl them with metal tongs, and two shades of brown dust on my eyelids. I am illuminating myself, trying to make my eyes look bright. But when I look closely at the actual eyes, the army green of them, I see an eerie stillness. There is none of the sparkle that inspired my mother to call me effervescent as a child, none of the fluorescent green and pink they take on after I cry. They are hard in a way that makes me want to back away from myself. I will know later that I am starting to recover when I see some light and motion in my eyes, a stirring, like a pinky twitching on a coma patient.

Most people don't seem to notice my vacantness, or at least don't comment on it. Most don't even know I'm suffering from PPD. I go through a stage shortly after starting the Zoloft during which I can't stop telling people about my new label. I blab to anyone who listens: *Oh, by the way, did you know I have postpartum depression?* I tell people I would normally be embarrassed to open up to. I must do it to elicit sympathy or reassurance. And listeners give it. *You seem normal,* they say. *I never would have known.*

I've fooled so many people because I do the things I'm supposed to be doing. But all my activities have an odd tilt to them. One evening, I drive to a meeting of the National Council of Jewish Women, an organization that once gave me an emerging leader award. It is being held at the condo of a new member. There are few condo developments in our town and I've never been to this one. I call Sheila, the hostess, for directions. I am to turn left at the Box Factory building, drive under one railroad bridge, bear right at the cemetery, go up a hill and see a sign for McIntosh Farms. A few more turns will bring me to her condo. She talks faster than I can write, so I only scrawl her street name after she explains how to get to the development. When I arrive at that point, all the roads and buildings look alike. I try to remember the names of the streets I'm supposed to take. Something to do with apples. I drive down a few condo lanes, but none of the homes bear her house number. The sun has almost set, so I can't read the street signs without stopping at each corner. Angry drivers pass by me, even though I am waving out my open window for them to stop and help me. I start to feel dizzy and hot. Trapped. I am disoriented and I want to go home, but I promised myself I would go to this meeting. I haven't been to one since Max was born and I'm supposed to be the emerging leader, for

God's sake. Finally, I pull onto a side street to call for directions. I haven't brought Sheila's phone number, so I call information on my car phone, an old model with a broken antenna and constantly low batteries. Then I call her house for directions, which her husband kindly gives me and which I neglect, again, to write down. I keep driving around the maze of identical houses the color of gray flannel until I see a row of cars parked by the curb. This must be it, I decide. I get out, but can't find the house numbers because everything looks fuzzy, as if I'm in one of those dreams where the world is blurry because you're sleeping with your eyelids slightly parted. I ring a neighbor's bell, and while I'm waiting for someone to answer, I see another member getting out of her car. She quickly finds the correct house and leads us in. The meeting is half over.

Another night, I go on a date with my husband. He has surprised me with tickets to an Elvis Costello concert for our fifth anniversary. The concert is outdoors overlooking Boston Harbor and our seats are close to the stage. I love concerts. I love Elvis Costello. I love my husband. He holds my hand and sings to the songs. People dance in the aisles. The air under the striped tent is warm and tinted a soft silver by the spotlights. I force a smile of thanks to Dave, hoping he doesn't notice how difficult it is for me to sit up. I am so incredibly tired. I feel like I have the flu. The music is only noise to me, so loud that my teeth hurt. When I stand to clap, my thighs ache. I hate every minute of this. The little me under the cotton smiles at the songs she loves, the lines like *I know this world is killing you* and *I would rather be anywhere else but here today* stretched out in Elvis's gravely voice. But the outside me is only chafed by them.

Even my relaxation habits are out of character. I am engrossed in ridiculous television shows. There's one about a nineteenth-century doctor with a sexy husband and many children, who performs surgery sans anesthesia on most of the people who pass through her midwestern town. There's another about a gang of angels who make mean, greedy, fearful folks nice again. Dave makes fun of me. *I* make fun of me. But I continue to watch these puerile shows that smooth down something in me, if only for an hour at a time.

I am functioning in society, though I have no idea how. I am like the widow who manages small talk with old friends at the party after the funeral. In the Jewish religion, the party lasts for a week. Sitting shiva forces mourners to socialize, only allowing them to retreat to bed for nighttime sleep. And for good reason. It's awfully hard to go off the deep end with a house full of company. When the guests finally stop coming at the end of the week and the widow is alone, she has been left with this: a week of survival. "I got through a week without him," she says. "Just maybe I'll make it through this day."

My days are full of obligations that are like little shivas to me. They force me to keep going despite the dire urge to stop. Between chores such as chasing Carrie around a dressing room as she tries on dresses adorned with cloth apples, and beeping my horn and flicking my high beams as a mechanic inspects my car, I make it through the days. I promise myself to hold on until the next increase of Zoloft or the next meeting with Kate or the first DAD support group. I must hold on. I feel burned down to nothing inside, but I can't let go. If I let go, I think, I will never grab hold of myself again.

Once, for one of the first times in my life, I allow myself to reach for a hand to hold. I ask a friend for help.

On a morning after a particularly restless night I wonder how I will make it through the day. The Klonopin isn't foolproof. Sometimes I still tumble through the night and find myself on the couch in the morning yearning for more hours to make up for the lost ones. I can't ask Dave to stay home from work again, yet I can't imagine having the strength to feed and entertain the kids for the next twelve hours. I search my mind for people to call. My mother. No. His mother. No. Kelly is on vacation at the Cape. Liz is . . . a possibility.

It is seven in the morning when I call her.

"What are you doing today?" I ask.

"Emma has day care," she says. "Why, what's wrong?"

"I'm not sure I can take care of the kids."

"Okay," she says, without pausing. "Just let me get my kids dressed and we'll be down. We'll get through the day together."

Her voice is soothing and upbeat, as if it is perfectly normal for her to come baby-sit me.

"What about day care?" I ask.

"Don't worry about it. I'll cancel. Now let me get ready. I'll be there soon."

It is a forty-five minute drive from her house to mine. She arrives an hour after hanging up the phone. Her daughter, Emma, plays with Carrie. Like Max, her infant, Eli, sleeps and cries for most of the day. She makes lunch for all of us, then orders me to take a nap after we eat while she watches all four kids. I can't sleep because I feel guilty that she's down there watching two toddlers and two babies by herself. But I lie quietly, feeling lucky and touched. Liz stays until Dave walks through the door. She has gotten me through the day and left a parting gift: she has taught me how to let a friend care for me.

The next time it is not so hard to accept help. It is a Friday, after lunch, and Carrie is at a friend's house. I strap Max into his stroller and push him around the neighborhood. In the best of times, walking and running shake loose creative and productive thoughts. In the worst, these exercises free the mind to snow with scary images. This time, again, it's suicide. Just the word, a mushroom cloud rising on a summer afternoon. I obsess and punish: *Why did I think that? Why can't I make it go away? When will I do it?*

I arrive home sweaty and fatigued. I put Max into his swing

and sit in the corner of the couch. I can't catch my breath. I can't go near Max. I am terrified of losing control and hurting him. If I can't control my thoughts, who says I can control my actions? Carrie won't be home for a few hours and I have nothing to do. The thought of spending all that time alone with my baby overwhelms me. I call my mother, tell her I'm afraid to be in my own family room.

"I have to ask this," she says. "Do you feel suicidal?"

Mothers always know how to cut right to the nerve. But I'm glad she's asked. Finally, someone's asked.

"No," I say, "but I'm afraid I will feel that way."

"Okay," she says, as if I've just reported that I'm hunky dory.

"But I'm afraid I will," I repeat.

I don't want to kill myself. All I want is to start living again. All I want is a normal day with my children. But I can't seem to get there. I'm slipping closer to the water, losing more of my hold.

"Let's think of something for you to do," my mother says, "Where's Andrea?"

Andrea, a good friend who lives a few streets over, has been consigned to bed rest for the last two months of her pregnancy. "She's home. She can't leave bed."

"Why don't you call her and see if you can go visit," my mother says. "Then call me right back."

I call. I go. Max sits in his car seat on the floor and I sit on one couch. Andrea lies on her left side on the other couch. We talk about baby names and postpartum depression. She had it after her daughter was born, she says. She stopped eating and sleeping for a long time. She understands how I feel.

I breathe deeply when the anxiety rises so it won't propel me into the ceiling fan of her two-story family room. Eventually, the clock tells me it is time to pick up Carrie, time to await the arrival of Dave and the weekend. I have made it, with the help of another friend. Sitting on her floral couch with the air-conditioning cooling her, Andrea has gotten me through those two hours.

B ut leaning on friends doesn't always soothe.

It is a Wednesday and I have been starting to feel better. Part of healing from PPD involves a rebalancing of the good and bad days. First you have one or two good days in a week, then three or four, until eventually you feel so well that you stop counting. My good days don't outnumber my bad yet, but they surprise me a couple of times a week. And when I have one I foolishly cram as much activity into it as I can. My PPD book warns against this, telling me not to waste my new energy because it's needed for healing. And healing is tiring. As the Zoloft starts to work, the exhaustion of breaking down is replaced by the exhaustion of repair. During this stage, I am even more easily overstimulated than before.

But today feels like a good day. I pack the kids into the car and drive to Liz's house. Despite feeling strong, I'm a little nervous because Dave will be working until eight at night. She's invited us to spend the day and stay for dinner. It sounds perfect: a day with a friend, one who will take care of me if I need it, and companions for the kids.

The day starts pleasantly, with the girls playing on the floor, the babies ga-gaing at each other, Liz and I talking on her old, torn sofa. Then Emma starts screaming, and no amount of cajoling or compromise will quiet her.

"She's had such a hard time since Eli was born," Liz says. "She just needs time with me."

They head upstairs, leaving me alone with the babies and Carrie. Whenever they come back down, the crying starts again and they head back up. They end up spending most of the day on the second floor. Liz is not comforting or entertaining me. She has disappeared. Carrie is bored. The babies need holding. By early afternoon, as I push Carrie on their swing set, it dawns on me that this day is not working out as planned. I'm working too hard, standing for too long. My friend can't take care of me today; she's got her real dependents. My daughter expects me to be her playmate. The babies won't stop fussing. All the children's voices make my head throb and the hazy sun burns my eyes. I have sensory overload, like someone who's watched too many sitcoms or done all her holiday shopping in one day. When Liz and Emma finally join us outside, there is no mention of dinner. When I say that we might leave early, Liz seems relieved.

At four o'clock we go, heading into rush hour traffic. Max screams in the seat behind me for a bottle. Cars surge then stop, their brake lights bouncing off my eyelids: on, off, on off. When we finally get home, I make Carrie a jelly sandwich and shove spoons full of gelatinous turkey and apples into Max. I am too frazzled to attempt the ordeal of putting them to bed, but I can play with them until Dave comes home. I read Carrie a book. I lie on my back, place Max on my calves and lift him into the air. I speak to myself in my head a lot, alternating between pep talks and despair. *I can't take this. You've almost made it! Everything hurts. It's been such a hard day, but you've almost made it! When will he be home? Good girl!*

By the time Dave walks through the door, I am on the floor, dizzy and weak, as if I've been in an accident. The agitated feeling is back. The buzzing in my head is back. When the day started, I felt anesthetized against this pain, but it's all worn off now. I tell him about my day and he sends me to the bathtub.

"You need to relax," he says.

He's right. But I can't. I sit in the tub, the inflatable pillow suctioned to the apple-green porcelain behind my head. I sit in the warm water and think of dying. But it's not just an ugly word this time. It's a feeling. Relief. The end. Never having to go through a day like this again.

And that's when it happens. That's when I let go, when my

troubled marriage with control dissolves. I stop fighting, giving pep talks, being plucky. I look into that hot pan of water and let myself drop. My hands open up and I free fall. In that space between letting go and hitting bottom I am more frightened than I have ever been.

I get out of the tub, put on a robe, and wait on our bed for Dave. It seems a very long time until he's done reading *Goodnight Moon* to Carrie and comes in.

"What's wrong?" he asks. I'm hugging myself. My hair has dried into snarls and peaks. I start to cry.

"I don't think I can go through another day like this," I say. "I'm scared. I think I'm suicidal."

It is the first time I have said the word aloud. He wraps me in his arms, lets me cry against his chest.

"I think we should call Kate," he says, reassurance in his voice. "She'll know what to do."

He's not nearly as shocked by this confession as I'd expected. Later he will tell me that he was forced to remain calm that night because there was no one else around to handle the situation. If he'd freaked out, then where would we have been?

He dials Kate's beeper number and tells her service that it's an emergency. We sit on the couch and wait for her to call back.

This is it, I think. This is the night I'll see what a mental hospital looks like. I imagine Kate meeting us in an emergency room and it feels comforting. In fact, everything feels safer now. Dave is taking care of me. I have passed my problems to him like the Wonderball and I am out. My secret is out, that horrible word finally spoken. Airing it seems to have stripped it of some of its power. Suicide. Big deal.

Now I am on the couch with Dave and a cup of passion-flower tea. While we wait for Kate's call, the obvious becomes clear and we come up with a plan. Finances be damned, I need some help around the house. Whatever it takes, Dave says. And I feel more relief. We talk about which baby-sitters we can call, whether the cleaning lady we once used can fit us in. The solutions are all so ridiculously simple. It's as if we've finally found the answers in the back of the math book and now our homework is easy.

By the time Kate calls, my crisis is waning. I wonder what she had been doing when I interrupted her. Was she at a dinner party, in bed with her husband, at the movies?

"I was feeling a little suicidal," I say. "But now I feel better because Dave and I have decided to get me some help around the house."

She isn't alarmed by my first statement. She doesn't mention a hospital at all, and seems pleased that we've worked out a solution.

"Have you taken your Klonopin yet?" she asks.

"Not yet."

"How much are you taking?"

"Half a pill." She's told me to take an entire pill, but I'm still scared of drug addiction.

"You need a whole one," she says.

When I hang up the phone, I swallow one yellow Klonopin disk. It leads me to a long, sound sleep. When I wake, I feel new. Taking psychotropic drugs isn't all I need to do to get better. Postpartum depression is a physical *and* psychological disease, but I had thought I could cure it by only treating the physical symptoms. Now I have leapt the widest psychological puddle of my life: I have let go of control. After thirty-two years of clenching my fists against encroaching depression, I have surrendered to it. I had thought acknowledging that I couldn't control *everything* was enough. Now I will learn that I can't control *anything*. And that's how it is for everyone, all the time. I've let go, and I don't sink to the bottom. But with empty hands, I am able to grip life anew.

Chapter 6

It is the end of August and I have been swimming for almost five weeks. Max is again playing happily in the baby-sitting room. Carrie is at nursery school. And I am building myself up.

If I stay under the water as I swim in the patch of pool that shines like an aquamarine pendent, I can pretend I'm in the Caribbean. The sea is warm and clear; a drink smelling of coconut is waiting for me on a thatched table. There is nothing to do at night but make love.

Then I surface, and I see what really surrounds me in this pool: fat ladies punching the air with their fists as they practice water aerobics; a man with lifeless legs being lowered into the water on a hydraulic chair for a physical therapy session; women with rubber shielding their hair and plastic sheltering their eyes who race with themselves up and down the lanes.

Despite my continuing exhaustion, I can now swim the length of the pool twenty-two times. My lungs and shoulders aren't the only parts of me that are gaining strength. Banging my arms and legs through the water seems to beat some of the demons out of my insides, too. And coming to the pool at the Jewish Community Center three times a week is like doing time in a halfway house.

I am being filtered through a minisociety from my isolation at home to the world at large.

Today, as on every swim day, I follow a precise routine from the beginning to the end of my swim. The lifeguards know me by face now. I sit on the edge of lane three, lace my middle fingers through the elastic on bright yellow swim paddles, and wedge a two-headed foam flotation device between my thighs. These are tricks I leaned from a tall German girl with skin and muscles so smooth she looks like a sculpture, though she's actually a nanny. For weeks, I watched her swim with the paddles and the float and I asked her, one day, why she did it.

"You go faster," she said. "And you get stronger."

So I tried it. She was right. Plus, I float. Swimming without body fat puts one at a disadvantage. Too much energy is used to stay afloat instead of moving forward through the water. With my ducklike paddles and the foam balls bobbing between my legs like a tail, my feet and chest don't sink anymore. I swim efficiently, my face rolling in and out of the pool to breathe air and blow bubbles, my arms cutting the water and pushing it out of my way. I feel guilty sometimes, using the props for swimming, as if I should be able to zoom down the lane without help. But these tools fit nicely with the motto I am gradually adopting as my own: Help is okay.

This morning I take off my accessories after ten lengths of the crawl, then do my other strokes: breaststroke, like a frog in a pond; backstroke, so I can look at the yellow-and-white-striped fabric pinned to the high, high ceiling above me; and kicking with the paddleboard, which lets me catch my breath and think. I think about the people in the pool, familiar faces now who make me feel as if I'm part of something. There's the boisterous old man with the gold Star of David around his neck who always talks to the leathery tan lady in the shallow end. There's the honey-haired female lifeguard who wears a wet suit and dives for toys and Band-Aids at the bottom of the pool. There's the strong woman in her seventies who must have been a swimming champion in her youth. *How do they function so nonchalantly?* I wonder. *How do they make life look so easy?* As my big feet propel me down the lane, I wish for their lives. Mine still tastes only of pain, with anger tossed in as a garnish.

The contrast between fantasy and reality in the pool mirrors my life as I ascend from the nadir. I fluctuate between the heaven of feeling like my old self and the hell of seeing only ugliness in every scene of my life. The kitchen knives don't jump out at me anymore and the oven door stays shut in my mind when I walk by with Max. But there are still anxiety attacks. And as if I weren't buried under enough stifling emotions, there is now a newcomer: a deeper sense of sadness than I've ever felt before.

Until I hit bottom on that night when I confessed my suicidal thoughts to Dave and Kate, I kept telling myself and everyone else that I was happy. "I'm anxious and obsessive and terrified of everything, but I'm not *sad*," I'd say. "I like my life! I just want to start living it again." Now, however, there's no suppressing my sorrow. I'm like an alcoholic who's come clean. Finally admitting that I'm depressed, finally tossing away the cap of denial, has made it possible to start healing. But it's also made the truth unavoidable. I am depressed. I am a depressive. I have lost the battle I've waged all my life. I have deficient brain chemistry. I am not in control. And that truth has brought with it a grief so thick that I don't want to get out of bed in the morning, or talk to my husband, or pretend anymore to play with my kids. The only thing I want to do is swim.

At least my body feels good. After thirty minutes in the pool, I head to the showers, spent but calm. My blood is humming and my heart beats with power instead of its usual skittishness. I rinse my suit, wash my hair, and grate all that is bad off of my skin with a synthetic scrubber. I wrap my head in one thick towel and my torso in another. At the locker, I put yellow moisturizer on my face and pink on my legs. Clean underwear. Baby powder. This morning, the benches are crowded with gray-haired, saggy-skinned women from the water aerobics class. As they dress in their rib-high underpants and polyester slacks, I listen to their conversation. This one's husband has gallstones, that one is going to Florida early this year, these two might try the new deli. It's soothing being here, in the company of so many grandmothers, but lonely too, because they never speak to me. When I finish dressing, I want to sit on a bench and soak in the wisdom and camaraderie they emit. But I don't dare appear that pathetic. I leave alone, stop in the hallway to drink water from a fountain, then climb the stairs to retrieve my son from the baby-sitting room.

Max is sitting in an older woman's lap, laughing. His care-takers love to hold him because, unlike many babies, he rewards instead of drains them. He will smile and coo at anyone. I pack him into his stroller and roll down to the café. We split a bagel, I sip hot chocolate and he sucks formula from a collapsible bottle. Sometimes people from the pool pause to say hello to us, but mostly we're alone. Still, I feel satisfied as I push his stroller to the car. It is nearly time to get Carrie from preschool. I have scored two goals before lunch: I accomplished something and disposed of half the day.

At home, I don't feel so sure of myself. I awake one morning in my blue bedroom and turn toward the windows. There are tiny holes in the cloth blinds that cover them, and the sun shoots through the dots like lasers. It is Sunday and I don't want to get up. When I was still denying my depression, I was hopeful on some mornings that this would be the day I would be cured. But now I am wiser and more cynical. I know the day could bring anything from peace to agony and I am always afraid to find out which it will be.

My good and bad days vacillate violently now. I have been on Zoloft for three weeks and I am up to seventy-five milligrams. The garbage in my brain is starting to decompose into valuable fertilizer, but it seems to do so in forty-eight-hour waves. I feel competent and stable for two days, then as anxious and obsessive as ever for the next two, which feels, in comparison, as if I'm getting worse. I am lurching forward, just to fall back. I wonder if I will ever feel better for more than two days, or will my life always see-saw between bad and worse? With that question on my mind, I wake daily to rushes of anxiety for the day ahead and intense sadness for the days behind. I never wake rested, either, though I am finally sleeping for long, uninterrupted stretches. I still take a whole Klonopin before bed. And I've started to sleep during the day.

At the end of the summer, we hired a college sophomore, whom we'd deemed too expensive in the beginning of the summer, to play with the kids each morning. Our regular teenage baby-sitter finished her job as a camp counselor, so she started watching them in the afternoons. For two weeks, I had only two hours a day alone with my children. While those young women in baggy jeans and clunky sneakers took over, I collapsed. All the parts of me that had fought to stay alive and upright fell back onto the bed, nearly comatose, while my brain healed itself. And that healing still saps me of any energy sleep might renew.

The sitters are back in school now, so the search for competent help resumes. I need someone to come in a few mornings a week so I can continue to recuperate. Maybe, if I find the right person, I will even start working again. Maybe. But for now, I need only to remove all stress from my life so the chemicals in those purple pills can plump up my anorexic supply of neurotransmitters. Today we are interviewing the first adult baby-sitter since we hired and fired Wendy, giving me a concrete reason to be anxious as I open my eyes to the morning's laser beams. She is being sent by an agency. I got the name of the agency from Jewish Family Services, so I assume it's reputable. The owner of the agency told me this woman has strong references and lots of experience with babies. That's why I'm so nervous. She sounds perfect, as if I could sign her up today. But what if I hire and fire her, too? What if I'm still completely unraveled by having a baby-sitter in my house? What if I'm not really getting better at all?

At eleven o'clock the doorbell rings. I'd wanted her to come earlier, but she said she had to go to church first. There are two women on the front stairs, both with skin the color of beef broth. The one I was expecting introduces the other one. They're both from the agency. The unexpected one has long hair and doesn't talk much. The other is chatty, but has a deformed hand, only two fingers curled into a wrist.

I ask all the questions I've read in magazines that you're supposed to ask. What's your experience? What do you do about discipline? Why do you like working with kids? Tell me about yourself. Then it starts. Church talk. They are Jehovah's Witnesses, they tell me, as is the owner of the agency. In their spare time, they go door to door annoying people. I imagine them bundling Max into his stroller and taking him on a proselytizing tour of the neighborhood. I imagine them singing rhymes about the bad ol' Jews and the good, good man named Jesus. The women are perfectly nice and seem competent with Max. The one with the stump hand gets on the floor and shakes a dog that jingles in his face. But he doesn't smile at her, which makes me feel less guilty as I lock the door after they leave.

"Now what are we gonna do?" I ask Dave. I've already started to cry again. Their agency was the only one I could find that supplied part-time sitters. No one has answered an ad we put in the weekly paper. Wendy, I've heard through the grapevine, has already found another job. My mother is still on her back.

"We'll find someone," Dave says. "We'll keep looking."

On Monday morning after swimming I hang a sign on a bulletin board asking for a grandmotherly type to watch Max. The place is swarming with candidates. The senior ladies are always flocking around Max, my Valentino of a son. Someone has got to answer this ad, I think, as I push him into the lobby. I stop to coax Max's arms into his jacket when a man in a gray cap approaches us.

"Vhat's his name?" he asks, pointing to Max.

"Max."

"Hey, Maxila," he says, his voice pitching higher. "What are you doing Maxila?"

Max grins up at the man.

"How old?" he asks, pointing again.

"Five months," I say. "Do you have any grandchildren?"

He tells me that he doesn't have any grandchildren, nor any children. He tells me, while we are standing with our coats on ready to leave, that his wife died four years ago.

"She killed herself," he says, "with chocolate. She had diabetes and she wouldn't stop eating the chocolate."

His name is Sol Weil. He speaks in an Eastern European accent, telling me about his life as a delicatessen counterman in Boston. He smiles and laughs a lot, and makes no move to leave us. It's nice to have someone actually stop and talk to me. A lot of people ogle Max and ask his name and age, but none linger.

"Where are you from?" I ask, trying to prolong the conversation.

"Poland."

"How long have you lived here?"

"Since 1949," he says, still smiling at Max. "After the war."

The date strikes me. 1949. He's older than he looks.

"Were you in the war?"

"I was in the camps. All the camps. Hey Maxila!"

Then his girlfriend, a stocky white-haired Russian refusnik named Lena comes from the direction of the locker rooms. I have seen her marching through the pool with foam barbells in her hands. Sol introduces her to Max, then I tell her my name. She eyes me suspiciously, not sure why I am so interested in her mate. Then we walk to the parking lot together. They stop to talk to another couple and Max and I say good-bye. I don't want to separate from

Sol, this contradiction of a man. So warm and cheery for a Holocaust survivor. I want to learn more about him. I want to stay in his company, because he seems both protective and vulnerable. I want to be his friend. So as we are driving out of the lot and we pass Sol walking to his car, I do something I never had the courage to do in high school when I was drawn to a man: I ask him for a date.

"Do you want to meet for coffee sometime?" I call through the rolled-down window.

"You buying?" he laughs.

"Yeah. When do you come here again?"

"We come Friday."

"I'll be here Friday!" I say. "Let's meet after I swim. Ten-thirty."

I am excited for the rest of the day. That night I tell Dave about it.

"I picked up a guy at the JCC today."

"Oh, yeah," he says, smiling too broadly, so I know he's worried.

"Yeah. He's really cute. His name is Sol. We're having coffee Friday."

"What was he doing there?"

"Just hanging out."

"Just hanging out to meet women?"

"He's seventy-six."

I tell him all I know about Sol. It's a treat to have something besides my condition to talk about after the kids go to bed. This is now the worst time of the day for me. Every night I sit on the couch, appearing to enjoy television, while I'm really worrying about the night to come. Though I haven't had insomnia in weeks, I am terrified of it. The return of sleepless nights means, in my mind, that this dip into depression is permanent. It means the Zoloft isn't working and never will. It means I will go crazy. I watch the clock until it's time to take the Klonopin. Kate suggested taking it a few hours before bed, but I'm so scared that it will wear off too early that I wait until an hour before I want to sleep. Dave brings it to me with a cup of water, like a nurse distributing meds in a hospital, before we watch a show about doctors in Chicago. My mind slows down during the show, the images of standing at the window at three in the morning puttering to a stop. When I go to bed I am not scared anymore, but I still don't trust the pill. I lie on my pillow and dare it to fail me. But it doesn't, tonight or any other nights. My rest is deep and full. Dave is still in charge of Max, though they are both sleeping upstairs now. Sometimes Max cries because he needs a blanket pulled over the mountain of his raised tush, or a bottle and the familiarity of an adult heartbeat. But not from my heart. I don't get out of bed for anyone now. The nights are mine and my body uses them greedily.

Two days later, Sol is sitting in an armchair waiting for us when I cross the lobby. He still wears the cap over his bald head. His square brown glasses are too big for his delicate face.

"Hi," I say. "Let me just go get Max."

He rises and comes with me, peeking into the baby-sitting room and waving when he spots Max. Max smiles back. He seems to recognize the man with the hat.

We order our snacks at the café and sit at a round table. Sol doesn't eat or drink. He's got a bad stomach. Plus, he's had a headache since the war. But that doesn't stop him from talking. He tells me more details of his life. He grew up in the Polish countryside with five brothers and sisters. His eyes moisten when he mentions the girls, all younger than him, who died sometime after he was taken from the ghetto to be a slave laborer. Only he and a brother survived the war, probably because they were hardy young men put to work in coal mines.

"We got more food there," he says. "But I still didn't eat. My brother, he ate everything. I couldn't eat it. I never had an appetite. I was always skinny. Like you. Don't you eat?"

I tell him I've had a hard time since Max was born, that I've been tired and haven't been eating well. Sol, as I will learn, is extremely intuitive.

"You didn't have a nervous breakdown, did you?" he asks, his forehead folding.

"No, no, no," I say, trying to laugh it off, wondering how he could have known. Is it apparent? Am I acting jittery or off somehow? Though I tell many people about my PPD, I don't want Sol to know. He's old. He won't understand. He might shun me if he knows how right he is. I'm not ready to give up this new friend yet.

"I know some women they go crazy after the baby," he says.

"Oh, yes," I say. "I've heard that, too. But I'm not crazy."

Lena returns from her swim and the conversation turns from intimate details about Sol's and my wars to surface chat about Max. Sol has been confiding in me and doesn't feel comfortable continuing in her presence. I'm flattered.

We plan to meet on Monday morning. I will end up adding coffee with Sol to my JCC routine, and it will round out these healing mornings. These people—the baby-sitters who adore my son, the lifeguards who watch me as the pool washes the debris of depression from my body, and the sweet man who gives me pieces of his pain and takes pieces of mine—become my guardian angels. I will come to live for Monday, Wednesday, and Friday mornings.

The next Friday I can't meet Sol because Max and I have a play group to attend. An acquaintance invited me to join in the summer and we've gone a couple of times. I'd thought it would be nice to meet some women with babies Max's age. All the other mother-baby couples live in a new development of large houses. They all have islands in their kitchens, counters devoid of newspapers, and clean, pale carpeting. Guests are asked to leave their shoes by the front door.

Lori, a thin woman with dark shadowy eyes, lives in one of those houses. During playgroup she usually looks at the floor and says little. But today she is animated as she answers a question about her job. She's hoping to extend her medical leave, she tells the ophthalmologist mother, but when she returns to her investment firm she'll have a new position.

"It's the job I started when this whole postpartum adjustment thing happened," she says.

I'd been listening to the voices only, not the words, until that moment. Then I blurt out my first thoughts.

"You have postpartum depression! So do I!"

I've told my story to people I'm comfortable with, but I couldn't have imagined admitting vulnerability to these seemingly perfect women. Still, I say it. I can't help it. It is like finally falling into someone's arms after months of running for help.

Lori tells her story: she'd gone back to work when her baby was three months old and was transferred to a new division. She felt immediately overwhelmed by her job. She worried all day about getting the work done and didn't sleep at night. After a few weeks she realized she couldn't cope and took a leave of absence. She continued to drop her baby at day care every morning. Then she would drive home, lie on a spare bed in the corner of her unfinished dining room, hug an orange pillow and cry for hours. One day she remembered the nurse who taught her childbirth class mentioning PPD. She called her, got hooked up with a therapist and started on Klonopin and Zoloft a few weeks before I did.

Then I tell her my story as all the other mothers listen silently.

"Wow. I can't believe both of you guys have this," one of them says. "It's good you found each other."

"It's great that you're getting help," another says.

When the playgroup breaks up, I follow Lori to her house. We put the babies on the floor and talk. She looks up quotes and statistics about PPD. She talks about all the books she's read on the subject. One of her coping mechanisms is to mow the lawn to sweat out her anxiety. Another is to read herself out of her depression.

"The library is the greatest place," she says, as if it's a speakeasy she's just discovered.

We meet there once, and talk on the phone often. We compare notes on therapy and drugs, energy levels and weight gain. There are two of us now, which dilutes my loneliness. Then I start learning about others. Kelly gives me the number of a dentist who had PPD with both of her kids. My sister-in-law tells me about a woman who couldn't stop washing her hands after her baby was born, an obvious sign of postpartum obsessive-compulsive disorder. I remember a woman I met at a prenatal aerobics class when I was pregnant with Carrie. We stood in the back row and goofed around during the class. She was the most fun woman there. The next time I saw her, a couple of years after the babies were born, her cheeks and eye sockets were hollowed out. She told me she never slept anymore and was always stressed. I couldn't even talk to her because she was so jittery. Now, I realize, she had it too. I am far from alone with this disease.

For someone who's never had kids, Sol is one overprotective grandpa around Max.

"Take it out!" he spurts one Friday morning, as Max coughs while chewing on a hunk of bagel. "He'll choke."

"No, he's okay. They always do that."

"Take it out! Take it out!"

He has revealed himself to me like a college freshman meeting a dormmate. First, I got the shell of his life. Now come the juicy details. After the war, when he lived in a displaced persons camp in Germany, he exchanged stockings for sex with German women.

"What about the Jewish women?" I ask.

"No, no. You couldn't do that to them. They were good girls. I wouldn't take advantage."

He fell in love with one of the good girls but he wouldn't marry her because he couldn't support her.

"I had no trade," he says, sadly. "I had nothing."

His eyes tell me that he regrets letting her go. He never had such love again. His wife was the daughter of the man who owned the deli where he worked in Boston. He had a trade then—making sandwiches and calculating check totals in his head—and she was a nice girl. But it was never the same as with the girl in the displaced persons camp, the cute, skinny girl, the love of his life.

"She was like you," he says.

I think about Sol's girl for most of the day, and wonder what happened to her. Did she marry for convenience, too? Does she still talk about the young man with the laughing eyes who left for America without her? It is a long day, with lots of time for imagining other peoples' lives, because I am waiting for night to arrive. Tonight, *finally*, the Depression After Delivery support group meets.

The group gathers at a hospital forty-five minutes from my house. I am to meet the others in a private dining room off the main cafeteria. I'm the last to arrive. There, gathered around a Formica-topped table, sit three other women. All are unnaturally skinny for their body frames, all are gaunt and gray-faced even though summer has just ended, all are somber. My sisters.

Karen, the leader, is heavy and happy, a complete contrast to the rest of us. She begins the session with her story. Ten years earlier, after the birth of her third child, debilitating anxiety set in. Antidepressants weren't used for PPD then, so they doped her up on Valium. She spent her days two ways: riding up and down the escalators in a mall for hours with her three daughters because she knew they'd be safe there, surrounded by strangers instead of alone with her. Or at her mother's house, crying until her father came home, then putting on a happy face so he wouldn't know anything was wrong.

The depression eventually lifted and she got on with her life. Her husband helped. Her mother helped. And now she wants to help other women.

"I know you don't think so, but you'll get better, too," she says.

"Do you have a relationship with your youngest daughter?" I ask.

"Oh, yes," she says. "I'm closer to her than the others. I think it's because of what we went through together."

She invites us to tell our stories. Patty got depressed after her third boy. She is so confused she couldn't find her way to her mother's house once, so tortured by impulsive thoughts that she fears she will hurt her kids. She hasn't found the right medication yet, and still isn't eating or sleeping.

"I'm not sure I can make it through this," she says.

Maria also got PPD after her third boy. She is starting to feel better, she says, as her Prozac kicks in. But before she sometimes looked out the window at her children playing and thought no one would care at all if she jumped out and killed herself. She had no feelings for her baby except relief when her mother took him away for a few days. She didn't eat or sleep while she endured the worst of it.

"But now my therapy is going better," she says. "My second boy had really bad colic and I was so scared this one would, too. I think that was part of what caused it all. And when I look back, I was kind of depressed after the second one, too. But not like this."

Lori, the woman from my playgroup, tells her story and ends with a plea to connect with other full-time working women who have PPD. The rest of us are at home with our kids.

"I have to go back to work soon and I just want to see how other working moms handled it," she says.

I go last. My voice shakes as I tell these strangers about the worst two months of my life. When I finish, Karen says we have to wrap up the meeting early because she has to get to a surprise party. I can't believe it. We've waited all summer to get in this room together and she has to break it up for a party? Is she kidding?

I want to stop everyone from pushing back their chairs and slinging on their pocketbooks. I want to lock the door and suggest a sleepover. *Let's all stay together until we're better,* I imagine saying. *We'll be okay if we're together.*

But no one even lingers in the room. We all walk to the elevator, then say good-bye in the parking lot until the next meeting, two weeks away.

Since I started my Zoloft on a Saturday, I judge my progress and up my dose each subsequent Saturday. It has been five weeks now. I can feel some difference inside my skull, a real physical difference. My head feels tighter, as if some swelling has gone down and my brain is anchored into place again. The morning after the support group, I take 100 milligrams, two purple pills. Then I say something really weird to my family.

"Wanna go apple picking?"

It is September. The MacIntosh and Cortlands are ripe. Depression or no, there's picking to do.

"Yeah! Yeah!" Carrie yells, jumping up and down in her pajamas. "Apples! Apples!"

Apple picking is like a holiday to me. All my life my parents hosted an apple-picking party for my father's side of the family. Every fall all of the aunts and uncles and cousins would pile into station wagons, drive to an orchard, and pick and eat apples until there were no more to pick. Back at our house, my father would bake homemade pizza for everyone. Mushroom and onion for the kids in the finished basement. Olive and pepper for the adults crammed around the kitchen table. It was a day of contrast in our house: my mother entertaining a crowd, my father bubbling with laughter, my brother and I cushioned with the love of our Boston cousins. Apple orchards are all goodness in my mind, like free samples of heaven. It seems sacrilegious to miss the harvest.

"Okay," says Dave, "let's go."

"Let's ask the cousins," I say. "It's better with more kids."

We take a picnic lunch and our nephew and niece, Sam and Meredith, to the orchard. On the drive, I start to get nervous. What if I have an anxiety attack? What if I have diarrhea? What if I need to go home and I ruin it for the kids?

The grass rolls and the trees are fluffy with green leaves and red apples, like a child's drawing. Dave carries Max in a backpack and uses a cherry picker on a long stick to get apples from the tops of the trees. I hoist Carrie and Meredith up so they can reach the fruit on the lower limbs. Sam climbs as high as he can go. When we tire, we sit on the grass and eat peanut butter sandwiches and drink fruit punch.

"I'll stay with Max," I say, when the others want to resume picking. "I want to take pictures."

With my old thirty-five-millimeter Pentax, I record the day. Click. Toothless Max licks an apple. Click. Carrie, in a pink hat shaped like a mushroom, plays hide-and-seek with her blond girl cousin. Click. Sam balances the picker with his long, tan arms and drops apples down to Dave. I pull the camera from my face and let it hang from the strap around my neck. The girls have started to chase each other. I pick up Max and run around a tree after them. He giggles, a sound sweeter to my ears than Mozart's flutes. I feel my face smiling. It's the second weird occurrence of the day. *Well, looky here,* I whisper to myself. *I'm having fun.*

Sol wants to meet Dave. We've decided to get together at the JCC café on Sunday morning after Carrie's swimming lesson. Sol is dressed more formally than usual, in a tweed sports coat and leather shoes. He kisses me hello and shakes Dave's hand.

"Ay, you got a cutie, here," Sol says, nodding at me. "Thirty years ago you'd have to watch out for me."

"I might have to watch out now, with all these dates you're having," Dave says.

Sol flaps his hand in dismissal, the way older people do.

"Ach," he says.

But it's not such a joke to me. I go back, sometimes, fifty years and imagine Sol as a young man and me as the young woman who saves him. He falls in love with me, but I don't let him leave for America. I soothe him of the nightmares that he still has all the time of Nazi's with dogs chasing him. I get to grow old with a man who talks to me about life's sore spots, a man who needs me as much as I need him, a romantic equal. Or I think of us falling in love now, at ages thirty-three and seventy-six, a Harold-and-Maude affair. And though I expect the image of smoothing my hands over his wilting chest will disgust me, it doesn't. It sparks something in me. Sol sparks things in me, things I haven't felt in a very long time. Tenderness. Excitement. A crush. Feelings, I believe they're called. Remember those?

Lena stands up from the table and pulls out a tiny camera. She poses us and snaps a picture of Sol and my family. When it comes back, it will show a young man and an old man, a little girl and a baby, and a woman with a broad smile and twinkling eyes who has just emerged from under a thick layer of cotton.

Kate, the other new person in my life, hasn't always made me as happy as Sol does. Though she has been patient with my infantile insecurities and repetitive questions, I don't trust her yet. Just as I have wondered constantly about whether the Zoloft is the right medication for me, I have also wondered if she is the right therapist for me. It's a common response from PPD patients. Because recovery is so gradual, we tend to blame all the external forces for not making us instantly well. Maybe she's not asking me the right questions, I think. Maybe she doesn't know what she's doing at all. There's one thing that's bothered me all along. She keeps mentioning cognitive therapy, a system for retraining thought processes. Her push toward cognitive therapy wouldn't bother me so much if she had a more balanced picture of me, but the me she's treated so far is much more warped than usual. So, based on the person she's treated for the past two months, she thinks I need a complete overhaul. But the relatively healthy me might not need it at all. Finally, on a Wednesday morning, I tell her how I feel about it.

"I don't think you can just lump me into a category like that without even knowing me," I say. "The person who you see while I'm sick with this isn't the real me. You don't even know the real me, so how can you say I need cognitive therapy?"

I expect her to jump back and return with something defensive, something that will give me a reason to never come back, to find a more suitable therapist. But she doesn't.

"You may be right," she says.

"I'm not *that* messed up," I say. "I know I've always had problems with black-and-white thinking, but I'm not a total basket case in everything."

She smiles at me and looks pleased, as if she's proud of me or something.

I come to Kate only once a week now. We have settled on Wednesdays at 10:40 because I finally have a regular baby-sitter. Nancy, a twenty-eight-year-old biologist from Venezuela, responded to our newspaper ad. She came to America to learn English so she can rise in the pharmaceutical industry when she returns to her country. She quit her last job, taking care of four children, because the mother was expecting another baby and Nancy didn't want that much responsibility. Still, her previous employer recommended her highly.

The first time I left her alone with Max (Carrie was at

school), I was apprehensive. But the fear wasn't crippling like when I hired Wendy. I worried about things that nag at most mothers when they close the door on a new baby-sitter: Would she drop him? Would she steal him? Would she be able to quell his tears? I have never worried that Nancy will replace me. With my mind starting to clear, I see her for what she is: a baby-sitter who adores my son, keeps him safe and reads the *New York Times* with an English/Spanish dictionary while he naps. It also helps that I force myself not to think about them while I'm out. Instead, I focus on therapy.

After my burst of assertiveness at Kate, the session seems to go smoother. We touch on the usual things: how many good days versus bad days I've had, how I'm coping with my day-to-day responsibilities, how I feel about not having the help of my mother or mother-in-law.

"Besides Dave, I feel like I can't really depend on anyone," I say. "I can't lean on them because they're both too sick to hold me up."

She tilts forward in her chair and says one of the nicest things anyone has ever said to me.

"You can lean on me for the time being."

"Really?"

"Really."

"Even though I was mad at you before?"

"Oh, Susan, of course. I'm here for you."

She looks to me at that moment, with her white hair and her flouncy skirt, like another one of my angels.

So I am developing a relationship with Kate, one that includes the many contradictory elements that define a healthy pairing. There is disappointment and disagreement, which I'm used to in most of my relationships. But there's also dependence and trust, two new flavors for me. Now I have two new people in my corner: Kate and Sol. Or so I think.

Sol's chair is empty on Friday. He always sits in the Art Deco armchair near the window overlooking the courtyard. But not today. Maybe he's already at the café. No. Maybe he's at the baby-sitting room waiting for me to get Max. No.

Max and I eat our bagels slowly as I stare toward the hallway down which Sol should walk any minute. But he doesn't. I stand in the lobby zipping Max's windbreaker, hoping that Sol will appear as he did on the day we met. But he doesn't. We have a regular date and he's stood me up. At least I think it's regular. Maybe he doesn't. Maybe he doesn't really care about me. Maybe he'll never come here again. Maybe I imagined the whole friendship. Tears pool in my lower eyelids as I push Max to the car.

I haven't cried in a couple of weeks. I thought I was doing so well, but here I am falling apart because a virtual stranger pulled a no-show. *I'm so damn fragile,* I think, getting angry with myself. But then I turn the anger toward Sol. How could he do this to me? How could he abandon me when he's the person who's been holding me up? Doesn't he know how important he is to my recovery, how easily he can set me back?

I can't take another loss. I know I can't, not yet. At least not until the medicine kicks into high gear. Or maybe that won't even help. Maybe I'll never be able to take loss again.

After I put Max down for his nap, I call Sol at home, to make sure he's okay. To make sure he's still my friend.

"Where were you today?" I ask.

"I had a doctor's appointment," he says. "Check the blood pressure."

"Oh," I try to sound as casual as he is. "I thought you found another girlfriend."

"Ah!" he laughs. "Another girlfriend! Hah!"

"Well, maybe we'll see you next week."

"I'll be there. I'll see you," he says. "Give Maxila a kiss."

So he didn't forget about me. *But what if he had,* I wonder as I load the dishwasher, *would I really have fallen apart?*

I get my answer Monday morning. As I walk though the lobby, I prepare myself to see Sol's chair empty again. I try to anticipate my feelings. If he's not there, I will be disappointed and annoyed. If he abandons me permanently, I will be hurt. I will probably even cry again. But that doesn't seem so scary now. It's just a feeling, not a fatal disease. And such feelings are just the terrain of the gray area, that healthy land between my usual emotional poles of joy and devastation. It's normal to be sad when someone I count on doesn't show. And it's normal to be relieved when I round the corner and my septuagenarian boyfriend is perched in his usual spot, waving at me.

I usually like Rosh Hashanah, the Jewish New Year. It's one of those festive, no-pressure holidays. There are services to attend and good food to eat. No fasting. No seder. But this year I just want to get it over with. I am standing in line at a take-out restaurant called Creative Chicken when I realize this. Tonight is the eve of Rosh Hashanah, and we are having my parents, my brother and his family, Dave's parents and his brother to our house for dinner. The traditional meal consists of good old-fashioned Jewish food, sweet and heavy. Apples dipped in honey to signify a sweet new year. Chicken soup with matzo balls. Tzimmis, a stew of sweet potatoes, carrots, and prunes. A roasted brisket for the main course and honey cake for dessert. I have made all of these things in the past and would normally be spending the day in the kitchen browning and chopping and boiling. Normally. But today I am not making this meal, in which I would take so much pride. Today I am watching a guy in a white apron stand behind a take-out counter and bag the food that I'll serve my family. Dave's parents are paying for it.

My mother is bringing the chicken soup and dessert. I am doing nothing but setting the table.

At first I was relived when the parents offered to take the burden of the meal from me. But now, as I balance Max on my hip and lug a paper bag full of food to the car, I am angry. And ashamed. What kind of loser is too tired at age thirty-three to cook a simple meal? It's as if I'm an invalid. It's like I'm an old lady recovering from surgery.

No, it's not, an annoyed voice inside me says. *It's like you're a young lady recovering from a disease.* Recovering. Disease. These are words I've read many times in books on PPD and from the DAD literature. All the wisdom on PPD stresses that it's a disease, not a character flaw. The experts compare it to diabetes, another disease that can't be controlled or brought on by bad behavior. They ask whether a person with diabetes would shun medication or feel embarrassed about her condition. I've read these words over and over, and they've made sense to my brain but not my heart. I still look for ways to blame myself for this problem as I have always blamed myself for my depressions. I didn't try hard enough, I forgot to be human, I didn't manage the stress of a new baby well. I didn't organize enough or nap enough or get enough child care. I drank too much coffee.

I have stopped telling people that I have PPD because I've become too ashamed to admit that I have a mental illness. The word *mental* is what I hear, not *illness.* Until today. As I get home and put the packages of food in the refrigerator, the voice in me rises to the surface again and gives me permission to rest. *It's okay,* she whispers, kindly this time, *you have been sick. You are recovering from something real. It's not your fault. It's not your fault.*

It's not my fault.

Yes, I've lost my game of tag with depression. It got me. But that's a lot different than being a loser. There is no dramatic event that jars this realization. It's simply the pressure of recovery, the progressive sealing of the brain, that pushes common sense into the proper slot.

Later, when I put the foil pans of food on the dining room table, I still feel disappointed that it's not my brisket and tzimmis I'm serving. Mine would be much better than this stuff anyway. *There's always next year,* the voice tells me. *Just shut up and eat.*

I don't count all the hours in a day anymore. They go faster now, so sometimes I don't even notice entire chunks of them. My mornings are filled with errands and swimming and meetings with Sol. My afternoons are filled with routine mother stuff, like play dates. At the end of September, I accompany Carrie to one for the first time since I got sick. We walk through the neighborhood to her friend Sarah's house. The girls play with a Barbie swimming pool on the back porch. I sit on a wicker couch covered with floral cushions. Sarah's mother, Carolyn, sits on one opposite me. We've been talking about Max and how cute it is that he can sit up and play now.

"You seem much more relaxed with him now," Carolyn says.

I laugh. "Why? How did I seem before?"

"You just seemed really stressed out about everything," she says.

"Well, it was kind of hard at the beginning. But we're doing better."

A few weeks from now, I will tell her that I had PPD and she will respond with curiosity and support. But I don't feel like talking about that now. Now is for enjoying the warm shade and the voices of little girls.

Afternoons are also for cooking dinner. We leave Carolyn and Sarah's at three so we can meet Jodi at our house. Jodi, the sixteen-year-old who has been baby-sitting for us for three years, watches the kids for a few hours one or two afternoons a week. Since she worked as a camp counselor all summer, she wasn't available until school started again. Her presence gives me time to go upstairs so I can fold laundry and watch Oprah. Or go food shopping by myself. Or take a nap.

On most days, before it is time for Jodi to stop playing in the basement with the kids, I make some pathetically simple meal, like pasta and jarred sauce or hot dogs and beans. But tonight there is a recipe cut from the newspaper in front of me. The counter is cluttered with ingredients: olive oil, an onion, tomatoes, black beans, potatoes, garlic, chili powder, oregano, and cheddar cheese. I pull my chef's knife from its slot in the block and start slicing the onion. Moisture seeps out with each cut. My eyes burn. I have forgotten to fill my mouth with water and hold my breath while I cut. I'm like a stroke victim relearning my everyday tasks. My occupational therapist takes the form of one and a quarter of a peach pill these days, the big 125-milligram dose of Zoloft.

The food is simmering in the skillet when Dave walks in the door.

"Look," I say. "I made real food."

"You always make real food, Sweetie," he says, after he kisses me on the lips, as he does every night before he even puts down his briefcase.

"You know what I mean. I *cooked* again."

He smiles, relief softening his face. He hasn't come home to normal in a long time.

A week-and-a-half later, I take 150 milligrams of Zoloft after breakfast. Then the phone rings. It's Kelly.

"Are you coming tonight?"

She has organized a dinner club that involves four families meeting monthly for a potluck meal. Tonight, the first dinner club, is Mexican night at Kelly's. I haven't decided what to cook because

I'm not sure I'm up to such a big outing. I don't like to commit to social events. Now that Kelly knows the truth about my lack of stability, she supports anything I need to do to help myself feel safer. But we probably won't be able to make the dinner anyway.

"Carrie's got a cold, so I don't think so," I say. "Unless she gets miraculously better."

She doesn't. By evening she has a fever. But so do I, of sorts. I really want to go to that party. It's a Saturday night and I've got energy to burn.

"Do you mind if Max and I go to Kelly's?" I ask Dave.

"No! You two go. Have fun."

The dinner club members have already finished eating when we arrive, but Kelly pulls a chair up to the picnic table for me and her husband brings me a drink. The rest of the adults kiss me hello and ask how I've been. Then I'm incorporated into a conversation with two of the women about pregnancy.

Max sits on my lap examining a paper cup and I sip strong, coffee-colored beer. The cool, smooth mouth of the bottle feels good against my lips. It is late September, but the night is warm. Above the trees the world is a soft denim blue, like the eyes of both of my children. Summer is over. But a tender sky makes one more appearance, possibly for me.

Chapter 7

Max needs a snack. He's seven months old, but he's never had a snack before. He's always subsisted on bottles of gray-white formula and three squares of baby food. But today, a bright Monday in early October, after I've spent two hours serving and clearing breakfast, dressing the kids and myself, putting Max down for a nap, changing his diaper four times, negotiating with Carrie about when to shut the television off, and finally getting us outfitted for a drive to the library, he starts to cry. *Now what could he want?* I wonder. He's dry, rested, and full of liquid protein. Then it hits me: he's old enough for a midmorning nosh. The poor little guy is hungry.

Off with the coats and back into the kitchen. Carrie takes a seat at the table as I strap Max into the high chair and tie a Pooh bib under his second chin. I spoon up three bowls of yogurt and applesauce, place one in front of each kid and take mine at a seat between them. Carrie digs in, but Max just sits there, before I feed him his first spoonful, and looks at me with a surprised expression on his face.

"Yeah," I say. "You get to eat now, too."

But even as he's gumming the spoon, he looks enchanted, as if he's noticed something new. Then I look at us, all in a row with bowls of soft food in front of us, and I see it too. Something is different here. It is the first time, the very first time since Max's birth, that we are a team. Not just Max and me struggling to get through a day. Not just Carrie and me trying to replicate the old times. And not the three of us somehow surviving with me clenching my fists until the day ends. Today we are a working threesome, a mom and two kids, just as I imagined when I was pregnant with Max. Not only are we a team, but we're finally playing our intended positions. Here is the mommy, keeping everyone's tummies full. Here is the preschooler, gobbling food and swinging her legs under the table. And here is the baby, messy and happy. No one is falling apart. No one is neglected. No one is sick anymore.

It's been like this all morning. We are sailing through the day as healthy mothers and children do, alternating between smooth and choppy moments. And it continues when we finally get to the library. I'm still acting like the adult and they're still being kids. Carrie bounces on the geometric foam pillows in the children's section, and Max crawls from pillow to pillow, sucking on them.

"Pick out a book," I tell Carrie. "I'll read it to you."

"No. I wanna jump."

"I'll get one. You can't come to the library and not read."

I scan the shelves until a pink checkered binding catches my eye. *The Lonely Doll* by Dare Wright. The most treasured book of my childhood. I bring it back to the cushions and sit in the center. Carrie plops down on the green pillow next to me. I start to read.

"Once there was a little doll. Her name was Edith. She lived in a nice house and had everything she needed except somebody to play with. She was very lonely!"

The book is illustrated with black-and-white photographs of a lifelike doll in a checkered dress and the Teddy bears that come to live with her. Edith and Little Bear get in lots of trouble, including raiding a hidden closet of dresses and writing on a mirror with lipstick. Mr. Bear scolds them and loves them. The bears promise to stay with Edith forever so she's never lonely again.

I own all the books written about Edith. As a little girl—a little girl with faulty wiring—I related to her loneliness and yearned for companions like the bears to save me. Edith was always struggling with her insecurity. Edith was always trying to live up to Mr. Bear's expectations. Edith needed some antidepressants.

Carrie's not as enchanted with the book as I was, which is probably a good sign. In the end, we borrow a few storybooks about cats before heading home for lunch. And I remain the team captain the whole time: confident and entertaining until the moment Max slouches over in his car seat to sleep.

I didn't feel instantly better the day I took 150 milligrams of Zoloft. But finally reaching the proper dosage gave me the presence of mind to hold on until I could see how effective this amount was. I stopped questioning Zoloft's effectiveness and I stopped panicking about whether I'd need to up my dose further. Except for the moment each day after breakfast when I swallowed one whole smooth peach pill and one jagged half-pill, I hardly thought about my medication at all. I figured if I had to take more in two weeks, I would. It was all part of my new mind-set. Instead of obsessing about "what ifs," I started developing a "who gives a shit" attitude about things that used to destroy me. It wasn't hostile; it was healthy. Who gives a shit if that blonde woman didn't say hi to me in the preschool parking lot? Who gives a shit if I don't make my kids' Halloween costumes? Who gives a shit if I need to take antidepressants? And within two weeks of ingesting the amount of drug my brain needed, I was well again, just as the experts had promised in the beginning.

With my head finally balanced, it's so much easier to work on the psychological issues that have always gummed up my life. Make no mistake: antidepressants do not solve any psychological problems. But for me, at least, they have filled the ruts into which I kept getting stuck. Now I seem to be able to traverse the terrain of my life much more smoothly. I can finally pass from problem to solution without tripping.

Which is good, because there are so many problems to address. The Zoloft has brought me back to my old self with the same satchel of worries, insecurities, and bitterness I've always lugged around. But the old me has returned with a couple of crucial tools. I've stopped suffering anxiety attacks altogether, even remaining calm as I sat through the funeral of our baby-sitter's mother. And I'm the proud owner of perspective, what I consider Zoloft's greatest gift to me.

It's perspective that makes me say, *Oh, yeah. I get it,* when I discuss with Kate the family issues I've gone over with all my therapists. I have always hit rocks when I dug into these problems. And the therapist du jour would help me move the rocks to a different place, so they wouldn't bother me. But then I would strike one again with the shovel a few years later. Now, I hit the rock, scoop it out, and toss it over my shoulder, gone.

"Just sit with it," Kate says one morning as we face each other in our black leather chairs. "Just remember how it felt."

The dog sleeps behind her chair. The sun warms my corner of the room. We are discussing a horrible dream I had as a child, one I've never forgotten. A man has broken into our house and is going to kill us. My father isn't around. My mother and I are hiding under her bed, but she won't stop laughing. The killer is going to find us because she's making so much noise. He lifts the bedspread and sees us. Then I wake up.

We spend many hours discussing my childhood. I want to figure out why I've always been so nervous and sad. Kate still wants to get to the bottom of my rigid thinking patterns, albeit without the cognitive thinking classes. She prods me to describe an unhappy moment, then stand under the downpour of emotions that comes with it. Once I do, I can dry off and move on. I've gone through my family crap so many times with therapists: yelling father, timid mother, anxious daughter. But I've always *told* the stories, not felt them. This "sitting-with-it" process seems to be working. With the ugly, once-buried emotions out of the way, I can see my history more clearly. It looks different now. Where once it was static, like a Fabergé egg in a display case, now I have broken the glass and taken it out. I can shift it around in my hands and look at all the darks and lights, the shiny golds and the flat blues. There is much more to see than I thought. Turn it this way and the father wasn't so bad. Roll it around and the mother wasn't always the victim. And from so many different angles, the daughter wasn't such a defective person after all.

Kate helps me to see this. She follows my stories with analytic epilogues.

"You were a little girl who never felt protected," she says after I tell her about the dream. "There were no real adults around you. No wonder you never developed a sense of security."

Ah, inner-child angst. The stuff of jokes. The stuff of truths.

It wasn't just faulty wiring that made me such a miserable child or the perfect landing strip for PPD. It never is. It also depends on circumstances. Having a mother and father who needed nurturing as much as I did. Being told how to feel, so I never learned to trust my own feelings. Feeling so out of control that I tried to control everything. Such are the psychic cuts and bruises that scar so many of us who are loved by young and fallible parents.

Later, I will accept and forgive my parents. But for now, in keeping with the corny inner-child theme, I must heal my bad old self.

There is a store down the street from Kate's office that sells beautiful tchotchkes. Hand-painted mirrors, boxes carved out of cherry wood, salad tongs of blown glass, and albums with black pages and white corner tabs to collect photos the old-fashioned way. For more than a year I have carried in my wallet a credit slip for eighty-four-dollars' worth of stuff from this store. Pepper, who continues to get weaker, gave it to me when she decided not to acquire anything new during the life she had left. At first I didn't use the credit because I had no idea where the store was. Then, when I would wander through it before or after my appointments with Kate, I didn't feel I deserved anything on the shelves until I cured myself.

But today, after all that work on my childhood, the credit slip sears a hole in my pocketbook. I weave through the small shop's tables and shelves many times before deciding what to buy, though I knew what it would be on the first day I entered. On a shelf by the cash register sit elegant pens made of fine woods. It's the blue one, the one carved from birch, sanded as smooth as an ancient stone and dyed with natural pigment, that I want. Around the corner I pick up its companion: a blank book covered in handmade navy blue paper. I have decided to start writing again and I actually believe I deserve to begin with beautiful tools.

The store owner wraps up my presents in magenta tissue paper and puts them in a glossy white bag. Outside, I cross the street at the corner and walk down the brick sidewalk toward my car. For the first time, I notice that there are trees planted every few yards between the bricks. I love trees now. My whole life I have taken trees for granted, but now I admire them as miraculous feats of engineering and artistry: their strong trunks, their permanence no matter what happens around them, their millions of flapping leaves like so many hands waving hello. The trees on this street are starting to look as if a child dipped her fingers into red and yellow fingerpaints and smeared them over the green parts. They are dying a beautiful death.

I love the sky now, too, even when it is the steely gray of a metal fence-post. Since the drugs kicked in, the world has brightened and clarified like a Polaroid coming into focus. The cloudy is vivid. The dull is bright. It happened so gradually. First I saw myself. Then my beautiful children, with their moon cheeks and comet eyes. Then red tomatoes on white stoneware plates. Now all my

senses are in on the fun. I feel the heat of the blowdryer on my
scalp, smell the bounty of leather in the shoe store where I buy new
loafers, slide a record out of its sleeve and dance to a scratchy old
rock song with my baby in my arms. I wake every Sunday as excited as if it were my birthday because the fat Sunday *Times* is waiting for me downstairs. The only thing less sharp now is my body. A
pale peach shade has returned to my skin and roundness has filled
in the sinkholes of my cheeks.

But my recovery is still in its infancy. Like the soft spot on a
baby's head, it has not yet been encased in hard bones. The recovering depressive should probably be equipped with some kind
of protective gear for the psyche, a helmet and knee pads in case of
another collision with depression. Because I run into it again at the
next DAD support group meeting.

I haven't been here in a month. I had to skip the second
meeting because it fell on Yom Kippur, the holiest day of the Jewish
year. Now I am excited to get back to the hospital cafeteria where I
can connect with my soul sisters. But none of them have shown up
yet. Lori, who is a step ahead of me on the recovery trail, has decided she doesn't need the group. But surely Maria and Patty, who
were basically on the same page as me at the first meeting, will
come again. I need them to come again. I want to see how they've
been, and to compare notes on the scut work of recovery: learning
to be well again, fearing relapse, and settling on medication dosages.

"Why don't we start with Melissa," Karen says. "This is
her first week."

Melissa is thin, pale, and jittery. As she tells her story, she
jumps from topic to topic, as if she keeps forgetting what she's saying. She is the mother of three boys, all under age five. The youngest
is already two, but she's been anxious and insomniac since the first
was born. She's been to several therapists and psychiatrists, been on
and off many psychotropic drugs and still feels as if she can't make

it through most days. Her husband, a firefighter, doesn't want her to take any drugs at all.

"So I thought maybe I have postpartum depression," she says. "And I figured maybe coming here could help. I feel kind of desperate. I feel like I'm never gonna be normal again."

Next it's Tanya's turn. She sits next to me looking like an overripe Concord grape that's ready to burst on the vine. She is about eleven months pregnant. Her maternity shirt is ripped.

"I've been through all this before," she says. "Karen knows. I had PPD after my first and now I'm trying to stop it from happening again."

She has reason to worry. She's divorced from the father of her first child. The father of the baby in her belly is an alcoholic. She's on the verge of being evicted from her apartment, which would leave her and her kids homeless.

"I guess I should make him leave," she says about her partner. "But then we'd have no money."

My turn comes last. I tell my basic story, then update Karen on my progress. But my tale pales in comparison to the others, so the focus shifts back to them. For the next hour there is talk about how Tanya can cope with the welfare system and with her partner when her baby arrives, which I'm sure will be before this meeting ends, and how Melissa can taper off some of her ineffective medication and get on something better. Time moves slowly. There is so much sadness in this room. I'd looked forward to an uplifting meeting, but this is a bummer. These women are a wreck. I feel sorry for them and want to help them, especially Melissa, because I know too well the panic over never getting better. But I am in no position to play social worker. And it's not good for me to be in a room filled with so much pain. I'm purging myself of pain. I can't afford to wade through it so soon.

By the time Karen dismisses us, my head is foggy. I feel pent up and cornered. I still get overstimulated if I'm around too many people or if I've done too much in one day. Bright lights, loud TV, and malls, where I used to find comfort in the neutrality and new-ness, still make my skin feel too tight. But usually I can see the wall I'm about to hit, and can take myself out of its course before I crash. Tonight sensory overload crept up on me. I should have walked out an hour ago. Then maybe I wouldn't feel so tense now. And I'd know better than to give Melissa my phone number when she asks for it.

The next morning she calls while I'm making breakfast.

"I just wanted to know," she says. "Did the Klonopin make your hands shake?"

It's a simple question and I have no problem answering it. Then she wants to know how much Zoloft I'm on. Then she asks about my therapist. I don't mind talking to her. It's nice to be able to help someone the way I wished I had been helped. But the timing is bad. I tell her I need to get the kids dressed and bring Carrie to school, then say good-bye.

She calls again two mornings later. I am stepping out of the shower when Dave answers the phone.

"I wake up all the time so tired," Melissa says. "Did you have that?"

"Oh, yeah," I say. And I want to add: *But I don't now and I don't really want to think about it.* But I can't say that. I remember exactly what she's feeling. She's scared and alone and just wants to connect with someone who's been there. Part of me is flattered that I'm the one.

But there's a problem with this setup. It forces me to look back on the demon that I'm fleeing. I'll wake up happy and her early morning calls will remind me of all the mornings I spent in terror. Or I'll be making dinner, relieved that I've had yet another good day, and she'll call to confess her fear that she'll use the kitchen knives on herself. After every call I feel tender, as if some-one is poking at a bruise. She brings to light my underlying fear that any day I will slide back to where she is. Mental illness caught me unaware once. Maybe it will again, just when I think I'm getting better. Maybe my relative health is just temporary, or an illusion. But I'm still determined to outrun the demon. And I don't have the luxury of looking back. My worst days are too fresh; too liable to catch up with me if I slow down.

I can't tell Melissa this, because she is more fragile than I ever was. At first, I avoid her calls. I ask Dave to tell her I can't come to the phone or I let the answering machine pick up. Finally, I tell her she should call Karen, the group leader, with her questions. She is strong, long past her PPD, and trained to help.

I've reached the last section of Kleiman and Raskin's PPD self-help book, which I bought at the beginning of this journey. I sit in my overstuffed gray chair, my legs hanging over the armrest, and read while Dave settles the kids into sleep. I have graduated through the words about suicide, medication, anxiety attacks. I have learned about roller coaster days and mistrust of recovery. Now the pages offer a bittersweet congratulations for making it. But what strikes me from these last paragraphs is one sentence: "Women with PPD have unquestionably endured a great loss."

Dave is upstairs singing to Max. I put him to bed sometimes now, but he prefers his father. And why shouldn't he? It was his father who blew raspberries into his tummy and held him as he cried. It was his father who saw him through his first step toward independence: sleeping through the night. It was his father who bonded with him while his mother was absent.

I feel as if I fell under a fairy-tale spell and slept for a long time. Before I went under, Max adored me. He clung to my collar like a baby gorilla holds his mother's fur. He looked into my eyes and smiled his first smile. I was his one and only. And now that I'm awake, he can take me or leave me. He reaches for me if Dave isn't home, but when he is, I am a poor substitute. When Dave walks through the door every night, Max turns up a light that has been dimmed all day.

"I'm like the nanny," I tell Dave when he joins me in the living room. "Max tolerates me all day, but he doesn't get truly happy until his real parent comes home at night."

"Stop it," Dave says. "He loves you just as much. And look at Carrie. She's totally into her mommy."

He's right about that. Carrie has shown no signs of maladjustment due to my lapse in mental stability. It's almost weird—as if she didn't notice her beacon had suffered a blown bulb. She never stopped trusting me or depending on me. Her devotion has never wavered.

But Max is another story. I have lost him, which is the worst sacrifice of this whole ordeal. I can tolerate saying good-bye to the confident mother I used to be, to the faith I had in my body, to the innocence of never having endured anything really bad. I can even take bidding adieu to Max's infancy, most of which I missed despite being there in body every day. But losing the bond we shared for the first couple of months of his life is nearly unbearable. My chest aches the way it did when I kissed my grandmother's forehead on the last day of her life. I never would have let my bond with Max go if it hadn't been wrested from me. I wish I could change that. I wish I could erase the time it took me to heal, and return to the relationship I owned before I drifted off. I remember sitting on my cozy blue-and-yellow bed and cradling Max when we first came home from the hospital. I looked at his minuscule face and realized that I finally had an uncharged male relationship. With my father, my brother, and even my husband there were hot spots, places where judgment or rejection or disappointment would flare. I felt I was always proving myself to or battling with the men in my life. But not with Max. He just loved me, person to person, in a way that was magical. And now it is mortal. The relationship has lost its neutrality. I want him more than he wants me. Unrequited love. I'm back to having to prove myself.

I close the PPD self-help book and bring it upstairs. It has lived on top of my night table, always at close range in case I needed a paper companion, since I bought it. Now I put it on the bottom shelf of the table along with the books I've never finished or haven't started yet. There is nothing left to read in it anymore.

The yoga teacher is tall and freckly, with a bonnet of red curls around her face. She runs her class in the family room of her house, a room lined with books on yoga and nature and healing. Incense burns and a tape plays music that sounds like bells. This is my third Saturday morning here.

"Stand tall," she says, "with your feet planted firmly in the ground. You are a mountain. You are strong and tall. This posture will help you to build mental and physical strength."

I close my eyes and concentrate. *Stand tall. Don't wobble.* My hands are raised above my head like a referee signaling that a touchdown has scored. We are supposed to practice yoga with a blank mind, but I've never been able to achieve that. Instead I use the ninety minutes of this class to let thoughts drift through my head. They start small: *What will we do for lunch? What should I get Carrie for her birthday?* But then they grow in scope. I have become more contemplative these days and I find my worldview changing. Where once I thought I had control over most events, as long as I followed the rules, I now believe in randomness. I had feared my breakdown, that ultimate loss of control, for most of my life. I thought if I got counseling when the anxiety rose too high or if I tried to be honest about my emotions I could avoid it. Now I know better.

"Okay, now everyone grab a blanket and lie on the floor," the teacher says.

The class is almost over. This is the segment during which she tells us in a tone as soothing as the ocean to contemplate every part of our body and relax it. She starts at the head and ends at the toes, but she loses me before she reaches the neck.

I always feel as if I'm going to fall asleep during this part.

When I was a little girl I would review all the scary things I could think of before I fell asleep. I thought I could avoid nightmares if I flipped through the fears like someone scanning records in a bin, that bringing them to consciousness would disable them. And that's what I believed about all bad things: if you consider it, it won't happen. But anything can happen. We are all vulnerable. There is no protecting yourself, no quota system: you've had your bad thing, so you're done. I had thought that once, too. I'd thought if you have one miscarriage, you won't have another because you've paid your dues. And if your mother-in-law is dying, no one else will get sick. But now I know the truth. There is no vaccine against tragedy. Whether you hold tight or let go, bad things will happen. Whether you survive bravely or die a little with each one, more bad things will happen. Whether you live poorly or well, offering kindness or cruelty, bad things will happen.

But there is a defense against these bad things: strength. I always feared the bad things because I knew I wasn't strong enough to handle them. Turns out I was. I am. My worst nightmare happened and I woke up. I survived this bad thing and I'll survive the next. I am sturdy, like that mountain the yoga teacher talked about.

"Now open your eyes and get up slowly, when you're ready," she says. She is sitting with her legs crossed like a pretzel at the front of the room. She wraps a shawl embroidered with gold thread around her shoulders and starts to meditate. We follow. At the end, she places her palms together in the prayer position, looks each of us in the eye, and utters an Indian phrase. Then she translates.

"Peace," she says to me. "Peace. Peace."

I take my last Klonopin at the end of October. I have been tapering for most of the month. Since the depression caused my inability to sleep, and since I'm no longer clinically depressed, I can probably manage without my sleeping pill. So far taking lesser and lesser amounts hasn't seemed to hurt me. But after my period this month, I had a setback. I went from feeling perfect to having ten days of mild insecurity and nervousness. Kate doesn't think this is related to cutting down on the Klonopin. More likely, my postmenstrual syndrome is proof that my hormones are still a little flaky.

I've been easing out of my drug dependence by drinking a cup of passionflower tea before bed. Passionflower is an herb that slows down the brain the same way Klonopin does. Last night I used it to wash down my pie-shaped quarter of a Klonopin. Tonight I take the tea straight, an hour before bed. Then I sit, as usual, and worry about whether tonight will be the night my insomnia returns. I will worry about that for a long time because I associate the insomnia with the breakdown. If it happens again, I reason, I will sink into the depression again. Eventually, I will only worry about it if I sleep away from home, with an unfamiliar mattress under my body. I will travel with my own pillow, stuffing it into suitcases or throwing it in the backseat of the car. I will guard my sleep time fiercely, never risking staying out too late if I can't sleep in the next morning. When I have to lose sleep because one of the kids is up sick, I will move heaven and earth to take a nap the next day so I won't start a new sleep deficit. Fear of insomnia is the deepest scar I will carry from this experience. It will take almost two years for it to fade completely.

But it is wasted worry, as most worry is. On the first night that I go to bed sans Klonopin, I sleep deep and long and wake refreshed. Which is a good thing, because today I have plans.

Kathy's baby is being christened. My whole family was invited, but I decide it will be more fun to go alone. At her baby shower, I was in tatters. Now I am sewn together. I want to celebrate my recovery with a day to myself. I wear a short black skirt and a new sweater. I stand in back of my bedroom door and examine myself in the mirror. I actually look pretty. I've developed a swimmer's body, with a tight waist and muscular shoulders. My posture is yoga-straight. My eyes dance when I smile at myself.

The ceremony takes place in an old church. It is drafty and dark except for the sun streaming in through stained-glass windows and opened doors. The guests gather around the stone fixture that looks like a fountain as the priest prays over the baby and drips a palm full of water on his forehead. In the old days, I would have been looking for exits at a moment like this. I would have been anxious and worried about the consequences of running out in the middle. But today I am only moved by and curious about the ritual before me. How lovely for all these people to welcome this child into the world. How universal the purity of water is across the religions.

Back at Kathy's condo, Linda, a friend who is a professional chef, prepares lunch in the kitchen. A bunch of us stand around waiting for her creations. The walls are brick and the cabinets are oak. I lean against the counter closest to the oven, so I get to sample the food before it is served.

"More salt?" Linda asks, as she hands me a spoon coated with winter squash soup.

"Uh, uh," I mutter. "Perfect."

When she serves, I gulp down the orange soup and the crab wrapped in filo dough. In between mouthfuls, I engage in small talk with Linda and her sister and a few other old friends. The meaningless chatter doesn't weigh me down or overwhelm me. It boosts me, to talk about the people we knew from Syracuse University or about the cooking school Linda attends. Where I once used to wander from room to room during parties trying to find a comfortable spot, today I stay in one place and feel as if I belong. I am a part of something now that I've rarely gained entrée to: the world of the undepressed.

When I look back on my thirty-three years, there are probably nine during which I wasn't depressed. Ages one to four. Sixth grade. Twelfth grade. Freshman and senior years in college. The year I lived in New Jersey. I was only clinically depressed once or twice during the rest of my years. But for most of them I was dysthymic: mildly depressed. I was almost always sad, or nervous, or waiting for the one thing that would make me happy. I always felt stupid and guilty. I always wanted to have a good cry.

And now I am just a woman eating hors d'oeuvres and laughing. It's nice in this world. There are so many things to enjoy. Just last week I ordered an expensive pea coat from a catalog. I've wanted a pea coat most of my life, but it never occurred to me that I could just go out and get it for myself. It seemed like one of those unattainable objects of my dreams, something undeserved until I found the answer to life's great mysteries.

"There is no answer," Kate told me when I first met her. "You'll learn that."

Maybe I have.

In November I stop counting the days. I had continued to count the good versus bad days until now. My record went from three good and four bad to four good and three bad. A couple of weeks later, I'd have five good and only two bad days. I don't remember exactly which week included seven good days because by then I wasn't keeping track anymore. I was busy living.

Which certainly doesn't mean that everything is wonderful every day. One night I sit on my bed and write in my journal about a particularly hard day. *"I feel so worn out and watered down. So unsure of myself as a mother and certainly a writer."*

I know it is time for me to start working again. I used to write a weekly column about parenting and suburban life for the local newspaper. When I was pregnant, I published monthly. When I got sick, I quit. I am afraid to go back to it because I feel I have to explain my absence from the editorial page. My readers see me as self-assured and funny. What would they think to hear that I spent my summer vacation being mentally incompetent? I am a little embarrassed by it. I haven't completely grown into my views on antidepressants and depression. I know intellectually that PPD was not my fault and not a character flaw. Still, lifelong stigmas are hard to shake.

There's nothing like hotel sex.

Especially when the hotel is new, and the room is decorated in luxurious hues of rose and gold, and it's been a long, long time since you were intimate with your lover. Dave and I take an overnight trip to Providence in early December while my parents stay at our house with the kids. We spend the afternoon poking in and out of the shops on Thayer Street, the main shopping drag at Brown University. We go from bookshop to coffee shop to trinket shop, holding hands and sharing discoveries. Then we head back to the hotel.

There are many people on SSRI's who trade in their brain dysfunction for sexual dysfunction. Men become impotent and women become inorgasmic. Though we've had sex a few times since I've been on the drug, I've never climaxed. I've worried that I never will.

But now we have the chance to test me. There are no children's coughs to disturb a crucial moment, no dog to rest her cold snout on a bare butt. There is only time and romance, which turns out to be a lucky combination. It works. It takes twice as long as it used to, but an orgasm joins the party. Dave doesn't seem to mind the extra work involved in coaxing its entrance.

"I'm starving," I say.

"Let's have a nap," Dave says.

"I can't nap. I'm always charged up after. You know that."

"Oh yeah," he says as he closes his eyes. "But I can."

When we're finally showered and dressed, we walk through the cold night to a French restaurant. We are seated in the bistro, a cozy lower-level room walled with stone. We order glasses of the house red, which is so fine it makes me glow from the inside out after the first sip.

"So, I can't believe I'm better," I say. "Do you think I'm better?"

"You are *so* much better," he says. "Believe me."

"What was I like?"

"You were still you, but sort of out of control."

"Like all the worst parts of me got worse?"

"Kind of."

"And now how am I?"

"Now you seem better than before."

"I *feel* better than before. I'm never nervous anymore. I finally feel like I have a grip."

"Well, it's nice to have you back," he says, reaching across the table to hold my hand. When the waiter comes with our salads, Dave doesn't let go.

The next morning my parents call. Max has thrown up once and he has a slight fever. But he's happy, they say, and has eaten breakfast. We are lying on the bed with the Sunday paper spread around us, the kind of thing we'd done before we had kids and will probably not do again until the next getaway. We are only half an hour away from home.

"Give him one squirter of the purple Tylenol," I tell my mother. "And call back if he throws up again. If not, we'll see you after lunch."

"Don't you think we should go home now?" Dave asks. He is already starting to pick out his clothes.

"The kids will be sick on and off all winter," I say. "When will we get to do this again?"

I don't feel guilty about choosing to snuggle with my husband. I don't feel like a bad mother for wanting to read the paper instead of clean vomit. I feel like a woman again, a sensation I want to savor for as long as possible.

The wallpaper in our basement is not yellow. It is blue and silver, a mirrored conglomeration of circles and loops put up in the psychedelic seventies. I can see how looking at it could drive a woman insane, especially if she was suffering from postpartum depression and was confined to the wallpapered room day and night by those who thought they were helping her. That is what happens to the heroine in Charlotte Perkins Gilman's short story "The Yellow Wallpaper."

"The Yellow Wallpaper," written in 1892 by Gilman after her bout with PPD, tells of a new mother forced by her physician husband to stay in a bedroom lined with gruesome yellow wallpaper while she recovers from "temporary nervous depression." In time, she comes to believe another woman trapped behind the paper is shaking it in an attempt to escape. The new mother starts ripping the paper down to free her. As she does, she goes so crazy that she thinks *she* has escaped from behind it, not the other woman.

I will not read this classic take on PPD until I start to write my book. But if I had read it earlier, I would have seen the connection between Gilman's wallpaper and mine. I am spending December stripping the awful mirrored film off the basement walls. I do not believe there is a woman behind it, or that pulling it off will free me of something. Only that it is ugly, like the last few months of my life, and I want as much ugliness removed from my world as possible.

With a thick orange sponge I slop a mixture of wallpaper remover and warm water onto the walls. When it seeps in, I scrape strips of the color off with razor blades. It is boring, cold, and wet work. But as I move around the room and reveal the simple white walls under the paper, I am filled with pride. Dave refused to help with this project. He said it seemed too tedious and time-consuming. He's right on both counts, but I am determined to turn this dingy space into a bright playroom for the kids. I love painting. With a can of pigmented liquid, even someone as artistically clumsy as I can transform a room. It is an easy achievement. Besides, it gives me time for contemplation.

Every day or night I eliminate more of the wallpaper. Before heading downstairs, I pull on my ripped, paint-splattered Levi's and a sweatshirt from high school. I tune the boom box to my favorite alternative rock radio station. And, as I do my work, I think. These days, I do a postgame wrap-up of my disease. *Why did it happen to me?* I wonder. I shuffle the possible answers like a con man rearranging coconut shells. I imagine that under one of them lies the reason for my unraveling. But will I pick the right one? Was it sleep deprivation or hormones? Was it family history or posttraumatic stress from the miscarriages and Pepper's illness? Did the birth of my second child dredge up pain that I, also the second born, had buried for most of my life? Maybe it's a little bit of all of the above. Probably, I will never know.

After weeks of stripping, the last pile of wallpaper dries in a clump on the floor. I am finally ready to paint. I sand and prime the walls, cover them with pure white gloss, and prep the trim. Using pink, yellow, purple, and green paint, I cover the spindles of the stairs, the shutters of the windows, and the sides of the square Lally column that holds up the house. On the last day of the last coat of paint, Dave walks down the stairs.

"This is unbelievable!" he says. "It looks like a magazine."

Indeed it does. Our bright colorful playroom is the envy of many a family. Crowned with new light fixtures and filled with toys, it is the sunny spot in our home. It is also proof of my return. Finding the energy to take on such a big project is something a depressed woman couldn't do. Jumping for joy as I put away the last paint canister is not the behavior of the mentally ill. Wallpaper, it turns out, is a powerful symbol in the world of postpartum depression. But in my case, it symbolizes ascent, not descent. As Gilman's heroine pulled the wallpaper down it became more evident how ill she was. As I removed mine, it became clear how well I am.

I am addressing the envelopes for a Christmas-day brunch when Marge Drake calls. She had told me when I gave up Max's day-care slot in the summer that she would let me know if she had open-

ings in the future. I never expected to hear from her again. I thought
she'd be too angry with me to give me another chance. But now she
is telling me that a child has dropped out and she will have an opening in January. Do I want it?

"When do I have to let you know?"

"Sometime this week, if you can," she says. "I want to give
others a chance if you don't want it."

I want it. I want it. I'd never changed my mind about wanting to resume my writing career. My mind had just forced me to delay it for a while. But now I want my life back.

I make plans to take Max and Dave to visit Marge's over
the weekend. Then I call some other family day care providers and
schedule visits. If I'm going to do this, I should do it methodically. I
will shop around before plopping Max with a stranger. I will not
commit to this unless I feel completely comfortable with the situation.

The first provider I visit is a kind woman with a filthy house
who plays with her charges in a basement all day. The second is
very professional and controlling. When I stand outside her door, I
hear her screaming at a child. Her house is spotless and her children
are confined to one small, neat area at a time. The third is sarcastic
and appears set up to do laundry while the kids play. Then there's
Marge.

Her playground, a huge sandbox full of swings, slides, and
a wooden boat, rivals that of the finest preschools. Her day-care
room, a large addition to her historic home, features red carpet,
white walls, and Disney decals. There is a merry-go-round in one
corner, a player piano by the wall, and shelves of neatly stacked toys.
The kids eat lunch and snacks at a farmer's table in a kitchen lined
with antique toys and animal statues. They nap in lace-curtained
rooms throughout the first floor. Marge and her assistant, Sharon,
share the work of watching up to eight children a day so neither
gets burned out.

Marge tells us all of this as we visit on a Sunday afternoon.

We are impressed. But it's a song that clinches it. Max sits on the floor with a Barney doll that talks. Marge sits next to him. He has never met her before, but he looks at her warm face and starts to sing the theme to Barney—*I love you, you love me*—to her in nonsense syllables.

"I can't believe he knows songs already!" Marge says.

I can't believe how comfortable he is with her. It's like love at first sight. We accept the slot that day.

I have two weeks to wait before Max's first day with Marge since she is closed for Christmas vacation. It's not nearly as long as the entire summer I had to churn up my anxiety the last time I had signed him up for day care. But I'm still nervous that these two weeks will set me back. I worry that I'll get so nervous that I'll back out of day care again, a signal that I'm still unstable. I worry that the insomnia will start again, and I'll need to go back on the Klonopin. But the new flexible me forgives human foibles such as midnight worry. *It's okay,* I tell myself. *You might need the sleeping pills because the first time you send a kid to day care is a legitimately stressful situation. It's okay to take one every night for the next two weeks.*

But I don't fall back. I find sleep every night, with only the passionflower tea to lull me to a dream state.

I drop off Max before Carrie. He explores Marge's toys with his mouth and hands, eyes the other kids, laughs again at the Barney doll. I kiss him on the head twice as he plays, then gather Carrie to leave. Max smiles at me and goes back to his toys. There are no tears from either of us.

I give Carrie two extra hugs at nursery school before saying good-bye. Then I walk up the stairs, where I used to feel so frightened, and into the bright winter morning. My hands are empty, my arms are swinging, and I can't remember the last time I moved with such freedom. I think of the command my father always chanted while teaching me to ice skate. "Arms up, arms up," he'd remind me. And I'd raise them to the height of my shoulders, gliding steadily across the ice for as long as I remembered to keep them there. I could do that now, I realize. Without a child sitting on my hip or growing in my belly or hanging from my coat, I have the ability to keep myself from falling. I want to stride across the parking lot with my arms spread just to sample this rediscovered skill. But I don't need to. I've already regained my balance.

Epilogue

Having postpartum depression was the best thing that ever happened to me.

Sounds crazy, I know, for it was undoubtedly a horrible experience. But it was also a turning point in my life. For almost thirty-three years, I lived my life under the weight of depression. For almost three, I have not.

"I feel like I have a new life," I told Kate one day this year. I see her only once every few months now, just to keep in touch and reassure myself that I'm still doing fine.

"I hear that from a lot of people who really needed antidepressants," she said. "It is like a new beginning."

Living through clinical depression was worse than the nightmare I had envisioned. I lost control. I came close to losing my life and constantly feared losing my kids. But, thankfully, I was spared both sacrifices. Then I received a bonus prize for my trouble. It turns out there was a blessing behind this curse. The illness gave me the opportunity to mend my depressive brain instead of constantly fearing its malfunction.

I think of the mother squid, the one who dies after giving life to her offspring, and I realize I am both exactly like her and not at all like her. Obviously, I didn't float to the bottom of the sea and die after bringing Max into the world, although a few times I thought I was close. But a part of me did die, a poisonous part that was sickening the rest of me. It was like a shadow that lived inside me. It took my shape and moved when I did and darkened most of the bright spots. It was responsible for the sorrow, self-deprecation, and anxiety. Then I got PPD, which acted like a fever to burn the sickness out, leaving only the healthy me behind. I clearly remember the person I was before PPD: anxious, pessimistic, full of excuses for not living a full life, angry. But I don't miss that version of myself at all. She is dead. Good riddance. May that darkness never haunt me again.

I had feared reaching this low point for most of my years, but it turned out to be my saving grace. Developing postpartum depression gave me the chance to hit bottom and start again. I now divide my life into three compartments: before, during, and after PPD. Before it was awful. During it was worse. After it is better than ever.

I am not gloriously happy every minute of my life, though I did feel that way for a while. The contrast between depression and balance was so striking that I felt high for about a year.

"I love my new short haircut, my new glasses, my writing work, my schedule, my dog, and my house," I told Dave one night after the kids had gone to bed. "I love you and I love the kids."

Eventually, I became accustomed to being content, so the giddiness faded. But I have never taken the other benefits of mental health for granted. I have perspective and strength and hope almost all the time now. Before PPD, such stability was a sporadic thing; now it is consistent. Bad things still happen, of course, but they no longer drag me to the bottom. I can cope now. I *do* cope now.

Medication is an essential ingredient to my mental balance. I had planned to come off the antidepressants a year after I'd started them. I still saw them as a crutch I'd like to be able to live without; still saw those people who didn't need antidepressants as stronger than those of us who did. As I neared my anniversary, I gradually cut down, taking smaller and smaller amounts of the pills every couple of weeks. Each time I reduced my intake, from 150 milligrams, to 125, 100, 75, and 50, I still felt strong. When I cut down to 25 milligrams, I began to lose my temper again. The week I stopped taking Zoloft completely, impatience returned. My perspective was wearing away. My behavior didn't change dramatically, but my brain felt funny, as if it were swelling and if I let it go for too long, the seams would rip again. My sleep was less sound. I began to wake up and worry about whether I'd be able to fall asleep again. I began to need hot baths and passionflower extract to get to sleep.

The old, masochistic me would have forced myself to go without medication until I broke again. But the new me had learned to care for herself. I knew I didn't have to suffer. I knew I didn't *deserve* to suffer ever again like I had during PPD. So, I finally accepted that I have an organic weakness in my brain, not a character flaw that I must flog out of myself. I started taking 50 milligrams of Zoloft again and have continued to ever since. I plan for it to be a lifetime supplement.

I can't attribute all my growth to medication. Simply having PPD forced me to surrender some of my most lethal psychological weapons. I finally let go of the control I'd spent so much energy trying to maintain. And once I let go, I saw the obvious: there is really no such thing as control. I gave up the myth that I was too weak to handle life's hardballs. I once thought I would crumble under any sort of terrible event. Now I know that no matter how bad life gets, I can get through it by just enduring the days until they pass. I survived my worst fear: losing control mentally. But I did not lose my mind or kill myself. I learned the value of being vulnerable. I did not lose myself because I reached out for help; I gained deeper friendships. Even my relationship with my parents is better than ever. They are not, as I had once judged, lazy or weak. They just have some faulty wiring, like their daughter.

I also started to make up for lost time once I recovered. I

funneled all the energy that had once been used to fight for control or worry about living into productive activities. I went to graduate school. I wrote this book. I took tap dancing lessons, until I realized no amount of mental health can compensate for a severe lack of co-ordination. I ran a road race. I made new friends. I bought an old house and painted the walls sky blue.

Life didn't return to normal instantly when the PPD lifted. There were adjustments for everyone. While I was sick, Carrie seemed oblivious to the changes in me. I had thought this odd because she is such a perceptive child. But when I was completely well, her sweet personality soured. At age four-and-a-half, she started throwing temper tantrums and telling me she hated me. Friends would say her behavior was a symptom of sibling rivalry, prompted when Max began to walk and get all the attention that goes with being an adorable one-year-old. But in my gut I knew it was something more. I knew that Carrie's anger was a delayed reaction to my checking out of her life for a few months, a reaction that waited until I had returned and she felt safe again.

On the outside, Dave only seemed happy to have me whole again. But his reaction to babies was bizarre. We'd always said we were "on the fence" about whether we'd have a third child. I was pretty sure I was done with the procreation game, but I thought we should discuss it to be sure. Dave couldn't even talk about it. He simply insisted that we'd never have another baby and changed the subject. He refused to hold other people's infants, even for a minute to help someone out. One night we went out to dinner with Kelly and her husband Doron in Boston's North End. As we drained a bottle of merlot, we got to talking and joking about Dave's fear of babies. He laughed along with us, but when he left the table to go to the men's room, Kelly said, "I think he has some post-traumatic stress disorder from your postpartum depression." We talked about it some more. Yes, it did seem that there was something exaggerated about his baby anxiety. But it made sense. I'd gotten all kinds of help for my PPD. My husband, who went through his own version of hell as he took care of the kids and watched me fall apart, hadn't even talked about his ordeal. All those nights of holding Max while he cried and wondering if he'd be parenting alone for the rest of his life must have been terrifying. When he returned from the bathroom, I suggested that he might have post-traumatic stress disorder. "Yes," he said. "I'm sure I do." After that night, Dave and I talked often about his fears and isolation while I was sick until he could again smile at a baby without his stomach clenching up. We then decided together that two lovely children are enough for us.

It may have hurt Dave to be in charge for all those months, but I attribute Max's mental health to his efforts. There are many studies showing that babies of PPD mothers have behavioral, cognitive, and emotional problems as they get older. The researchers attribute the problems to living with a depressed mother who doesn't engage in eye contact or give the baby the comfort he needs.

But Max would skew those studies. Besides being rather mischievous, he is an extremely well-adjusted, smart little kid. Because his dad looked in his eyes and told him about his day, tickled his chin and rolled balls to him, Max wasn't lacking in paternal contact. I believe Dave's attention every morning and night made up for all I couldn't give during the day.

Until Max was about two, he still clearly preferred Dave to me. He would call for "Dada," every morning when he woke up. His face would drop with disappointment when I entered the room, even when I sang for him and danced around his crib. But gradually it began to change. He'd started tracking me.

"Where Mama?" he'd ask Dave the minute I left a room. "Mama sleeping?" he'd ask as he sipped his morning juice with Dave. Then, when he heard the toilet flush and my footsteps heading toward the stairs, his eyes would illuminate and he'd yell, "Mommy!"

But I knew I had him back when the ducks invaded his bedroom.

It was three in the morning when I heard his scream, a silence-slicing bellow that drew me to his crib side before I realized I was awake. He sat up when he saw me.

"My scared!" he cried.

He'd had a nightmare, the kind of awful dreams that blossom in the dark from a seed planted in the day.

"Come here, Sweetie," I said, "Mommy's here. You come to Mommy's bed."

I was sure he would roll toward Dave the minute I placed him on the mattress between our pillows, but he didn't. He crouched by my side and put his head and torso over my heart. One fist clenched my pajama top so tightly I could have swung from a tree and not dropped him. His other arm and hand were woven through my elbow. If I tried to move, he clung tighter. It was hours before I could lift him off my chest and settle him next to me.

"Don't you want to lie with Daddy?" I asked.

"No!" Max said, suddenly and firmly, case closed.

I didn't sleep much that night, but I didn't mind. I had my baby back, my little boy, wrapped around me as tightly as when he drew life from me. The PPD hadn't severed our connection. It had just been an interruption, a call-waiting in a long phone conversation. The next morning, Max told me what had woken him up.

"Ducks in my droom," he said.

A room full of ducks. That would scare anyone into his mother's arms. Thank God.

A year later, our bond remains strong. When we arrive at Marge's for day care, he scampers for the toys and I talk with her for a minute. Then I prepare to leave. He runs back to me.

"A hug and a kiss!" he says, as he cradles my head in his arms and kisses my cheek again and again, wet, warm smooches that don't dry until I'm halfway home.

. . .

It is said that the first year after the death of someone close is the hardest because the survivors must live through all the significant events without the deceased. My first year after PPD was similarly painful, especially the next summer. Every time I returned to the scene of a particularly bad day, such as the lake, or felt the same temperature as those worst weeks brush my bare arm, the bitter memories returned. One day I ironed a load of clothes so I could sell them to a consignment shop. As I put them in a pile, I noticed that most of them were from the spring and summer of PPD. Had I chosen to sell them, I wondered, because they reeked of sadness or because I simply didn't like them? They certainly reflected how absent I had been during those months. It was as if someone else had chosen the silk blouse the color of purple Easter eggs or the hot-pink tank dress, clothes so far from my normal taste.

As I ironed each sleeve, collar, and seam, the memories of that year rose up to me like the steam that erased the wrinkles. Every event to which a garment was worn returned in Technicolor. Dave's cousin's wedding, where I cried over spilling my pumped breast milk down the drain; Andrea's graduation party, from which I drove home believing my life revolved around the cries of babies; a Passover seder during which I spent most of the time upstairs, nursing, listening through a haze of exhaustion as others enjoyed themselves. It hurt to relive these scenes, but I made myself watch them and feel them, because I knew that was the only way they would fade.

The most lingering scar from my PPD experience was my fear of insomnia. I still blamed my breakdown on sleep deprivation and associated insomnia with the ultimate loss of control. If I suffered insomnia again, I reasoned, I would get depressed again. To protect myself, I packed half a Klonopin and a relaxation tape for insomniacs whenever I went on vacation, in case I needed them to sleep. I never used the pills and only listened to the tape once, in a stuffy room in a New Hampshire bed and breakfast. Still, I feared a severe loss of sleep. Then I had one.

Max contracted a rare illness called Kawasaki disease when he was two. Kawasaki, the major cause of childhood heart disease in this country, causes the vascular system to swell. Thankfully, Max was treated for the disease in time and his heart stayed strong and healthy. But it took a week in the hospital for the doctors to diagnose, then treat him with gamma globulin. I lay with him in a hospital bed every night, though I rarely slept. Nurses barged in to check his temperature or change his IV bags. He awoke to vomit all over the sheets. He moaned and clung to me as his fever and rash worsened. I was too busy worrying about Max to think much about my sleep status. But when he had recovered, I realized that I had essentially not slept for a week. My mind had stayed strong. I wasn't depressed or even irrational. That's when I realized that sleep deprivation and depression are not always linked. That's when I tossed away my terror of sleepless nights and sleepless days. That's when I knew I was all better.

To learn more about postpartum depression, find a support group, or get a referral to a mental health practitioner who specializes in PPD, please contact:

Depression After Delivery (DAD): 1-800-944-4773
Postpartum Support International (PSI): 805-967-7636

You can also obtain information about local DAD support groups and PPD therapists by contacting childbirth educators and breast pump rental agencies in your area. Your OB-GYN or the hospital at which your baby was born should also be able to point you in the right direction.

About the Author

SUSAN KUSHNER RESNICK worked as a reporter for various weekly and daily newspapers before becoming a freelance writer. Her work has appeared in the "Hers" column of *The New York Times Magazine, Natural Health,* and other periodicals. She is currently working toward an MFA degree in creative nonfiction. She lives outside of Boston with her husband and two children.